WORLD WAR II

Countdown to Catastrophe

Marshall Cavendish
Benchmark
New York

Website: www.marshallcavendish.us

This publication represents the opinions and views of the authors based on the authors' personal experience, knowledge, and research. The information in this book serves as a general guide only. The authors and publisher have used their best efforts in preparing this book and disclaim liability rising directly and indirectly from the use and application of this book.

Other Marshall Cavendish Offices:
Marshall Cavendish International (Asia) Private Limited, 1 New Industrial Road, Singapore 536196 • Marshall Cavendish International (Thailand) Co Ltd. 253 Asoke, 12th Flr, Sukhumvit 21 Road, Klongtoey Nua, Wattana, Bangkok 10110, Thailand • Marshall Cavendish (Malaysia) Sdn Bhd, Times Subang, Lot 46, Subang Hi-Tech Industrial Park, Batu Tiga, 40000 Shah Alam, Selangor Darul Ehsan, Malaysia

Marshall Cavendish is a trademark of Times Publishing Limited

All websites were available and accurate when this book was sent to press.

Library of Congress Cataloging-in-Publication Data

Countdown to catastrophe.
    p. cm. -- (World War II)
  Summary: "Covers the aftermath of World War I and events in Europe, Asia, Africa, the Middle East, and the U.S. from 1919 to 1939 which lead to the outbreak of World War II"--Provided by publisher.
  Includes bibliographical references and index.
  ISBN 978-0-7614-4944-7
  1. World War, 1939-1945--Causes--Juvenile literature. 2. World War, 1914-1918--Influence--Juvenile literature. 3. World politics--1919-1932--Juvenile literature. 4. World politics--1933-1945--Juvenile literature.
  D741.C68 2011
  940.53'11--dc22
                          2010008619
Senior Editor: Deborah Grahame-Smith
Publisher: Michelle Bisson
Art Director: Anahid Hamparian
Series Designer: Bill Smith Group

PICTURE CREDITS
Associated Press: 19, 20, 29, 42, 54, 64, 70, 77, 95, 107.
Dreamstime: 86.
Library of Congress: 4 (U.S. Army Signal Corps.), 7, 11 (Frank and Frances Carpenter Collection), 13 (Harris & Ewing), 16 (Underwood & Underwood/J.F. Jarvis, publisher), 22-23 (W. L. King, October 19, 1921), 24 (Harris & Ewing Collection), 25, 27, 31, 32, 36 (George Grantham Bain Collection), 39 (International News Photos, Inc.), 44 (Russell Lee, photographer), 46 (Dorothea Lange, photographer), 50 (Arthur Rothstein, photographer), 73 (U.S. News & World Report Magazine Photograph Collection), 74, 91 (G. Eric and Edith Matson Photograph Collection), 93 (Underwood & Underwood), 96 (National Photo Company Collection), 113, 115 (George Grantham Bain Collection).
NAVY Amphibious Photo Archive: 12 (Darryl Baker, contributor).
Robert Hunt Library: Cover c, 1,14, 52, 68, 82, 102, 110, 116
Shutterstock: Cover bkgd (Ozgur Artug), 3l (Andi Berger), 3r (Jim Barber), 61 (Scotshot), 79 (Sergey Kamshylin), 104 (Mark Yuill).

Additional imagery provided by U.S. Army, Joseph Gary Sheahan, 1944, Dreamstime.com, Shutterstock.com.

Printed in Malaysia (T)
135642

Contents

▶ U.S. Army infantry troops, African–American unit, marching near Verdun, France, in World War I.

1 Legacies of World War I

KEY PEOPLE	KEY PLACES
✳ Adolf Hitler	☪ Constantinople, Turkey
▬ Miklós Horthy	🇫🇷 Paris, France
☪ Mustafa Kemal (Kemal Atatürk)	🇺🇸 Washington, D.C.
🇺🇸 Woodrow Wilson	

World War I, in the eyes of Britain, France, and the United States, was supposed to be the "war to end all wars." Unfortunately, this prediction did not come true. The 1914 to 1918 war was originally called the "Great War." This was because no one could imagine a worse war happening again. It was also the war that was fought "to make the world safe for democracy."

The hopes of 1918 were dashed by 1939. In looking back at this time period, it becomes clear that World War II was not so much a new war as a second act of the Great War. But unlike World War I, World War II was truly a world war. The battlefields of World War I were mostly in Europe. But World War II battlefields included not only Europe but also East, Southeast and South Asia, the Pacific, North Africa, and the Near East.

The Global Perspective

The world in 1919 was very different from the world in 1914. Three previously powerful empires, Germany, Austria-Hungary, and Ottoman Turkey, no longer existed. Germany lost its overseas colonies. The Austro-Hungarian Empire and the Turkish (Ottoman) Empire fell.

France and Britain were on the winning side in World War I, so they kept their overseas empires. But their power had weakened. The world's future seemed to depend on two countries, the United States and Russia. The United States had become the world's greatest economic and military power. Under Communist control since 1917, Russia was no longer industrially backward.

At the Paris Peace Conference in 1919, Russia lost large territories to Poland, Czechoslovakia, and Romania. In addition, independent democratic republics were formed in Finland, Estonia, Latvia, and Lithuania.

The creation of republics seemed to be the way of the future. Almost all the new countries formed after World War I wrote constitutions. The monarchies of Russia, Austria-Hungary, and Germany disappeared. Only in the Islamic Near East did imperial forms of government, or monarchies, continue.

The Treaty of Versailles redrew the map of Europe. Germany lost territory to Poland, Belgium, Denmark, and France.

At the same time, nationalism was on the rise. U.S. president Woodrow Wilson's Fourteen Points encouraged nationalism. Wilson thought that all cultural groups should control their own independent nations.

In the Middle East, too, the war had strengthened nationalism. The Ottoman Empire ruled Arab peoples in much of the Middle East. Britain and France encouraged the Arabs to revolt against the Ottomans in 1916 and promised to grant the Arabs independence. But after the war, Britain and France took control of the Arab areas through League of Nations' mandates. The British government also promised to support a Jewish homeland in Palestine, an Arab country.

As the peace conference met, the biggest question was what would happen to Europe. The people and governments of the continent were exhausted by war. Could they rebuild? In particular, could Germany become a stable, democratic, peaceful country?

POLITICAL WORLD — WILSON'S FOURTEEN POINTS

In 1918, U. S. president Woodrow Wilson proposed his Fourteen Points. He wanted these to be the basis for the peace agreements when World War I ended. His first five points were general principles:

- No secret diplomacy
- Freedom of ships to travel on the seas outside territorial waters
- Removal of barriers to free trade
- Reduction of weapons
- Fair consideration of colonial requests for independence

Points six to thirteen related to European boundaries. Wilson believed that every cultural group had the right of national self-determination. This idea supported the creation of new countries in Europe. Wilson's last point called for "a general association of nations." This became the League of Nations.

Woodrow Wilson was the twenty-eighth U.S. president. He served from 1913 to 1921.

The Treaty of Versailles

World War I ended on November 11, 1918. This date is called Armistice Day. In January 1919 the winning countries met in Paris. They drew up peace treaties with each of the defeated countries: Germany, Austria, Hungary, Bulgaria, and Turkey. The defeated countries were not allowed to take part. Russia was also excluded.

Britain and France wanted to punish Germany. They demanded that Germany pay heavily for the war.

Britain, France, and the United States were the leaders at the conference. Britain and France wanted to punish Germany. They demanded that Germany pay heavily for the war. U. S. president Woodrow Wilson wrote a list of Fourteen Points. He thought these points should be the foundation of a peace agreement. Harshly punishing Germany, Wilson thought, would make the German people want revenge. In the end, Britain and France largely won this argument. President Wilson was disappointed.

The treaty with Germany was called the Treaty of Versailles. It was signed in June 1919. The terms of the treaty were harsh. Germany was

This chart shows the combat losses suffered by the major participants of World War I.

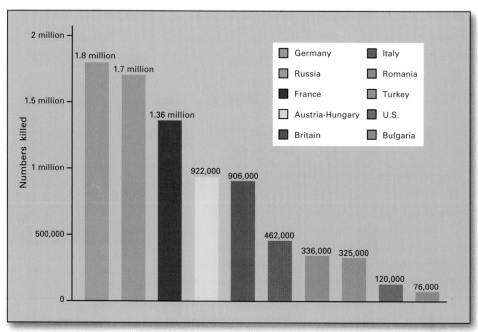

forced to officially take the blame for the outbreak of the war. This helped France and Britain to justify the harsh treatment of Germany.

Germany lost territory to a reformed and independent Poland. Alsace-Lorraine, which was lost in a previous war, was returned to France. The territory of Saarland, with its many factories and mines, was placed under the management of the League of Nations for fifteen years.

The treaty took away all of Germany's overseas colonies. Any future unification with Austria was forbidden. Germany could not have a large army or navy. It was not allowed to have an air force at all.

In all, Germany lost about 13 percent of its land, 10 percent of its population, 75 percent of its iron ore, and 25 percent of its best coal mines. These losses hurt the German economy badly. At the same time, the treaty required Germany to pay $3.3 billion to the Allies. This debt, known as reparations, created a massive economic obstacle to Germany's attempts to rebuild.

The people of Germany resented the treaty. This resentment played into the hands of right-wing, nationalist politicians. One such politician was Adolf Hitler, leader of the National Socialists (Nazis).

POLITICAL WORLD — THE DAWES AND YOUNG PLANS

From the start, Germany could not keep up with its reparations debt. In 1923, Germany defaulted on its debt. In response, the Allies created a committee in 1924 headed by a U.S. banker named Charles Dawes. The Dawes Plan did not reduce the German debt, but it did spread out its payments. It also provided a large loan to Germany. This helped the German economy improve in the late 1920s.

In 1929 there was a second agreement, called the Young Plan. This plan was named after Owen Young, a U.S. diplomat. This plan gave Germany another large loan and spread reparations payments out over the next fifty-nine years.

Finally, in June 1932, an international conference agreed to forgive all of Germany's remaining reparations debt. However, the reparations issue had already stirred up resentment among Germans. They felt that the Allies had punished them unfairly, and this feeling assisted the Nazis in their rise to power.

The League of Nations

Member nations agreed to settle their differences by talking, not fighting. They also agreed to help protect any fellow member country that was attacked.

The Treaty of Versailles called for the creation of a League of Nations. This was one of Woodrow Wilson's Fourteen Points. The League would be a forum where countries could settle their disputes without war. The League would meet in Switzerland, a neutral country. (Switzerland did not join either side in the Great War.)

Member nations agreed to settle their differences by talking, not fighting. They also agreed to help protect any fellow member country that was attacked. If all else failed, the League had the right to use military force to stop a country that was attacking a neighbor.

The League would also protect ethnic minorities and supervise lands known as mandates. These mandates included Germany's former colonies and former territories of the Ottoman Empire.

At first, only Allied countries belonged to the League. Some countries never joined. Eventually Germany joined in 1926, but the Nazis took Germany out in 1933. The Soviet Union did not join until 1934. The United States never joined, even though the League was President Wilson's idea. The lack of U.S. membership made the League weaker.

In the 1930s, when Italy and Japan began to attack weaker countries, the League turned out to be too weak to stop them. With no army of its own, the League could not enforce its decisions. The idea of an international body working to keep peace became the basis for the United Nations after World War II.

With no army of its own, the League could not enforce its decisions.

There were other efforts to keep peace. In 1928, sixty-five countries signed the Kellogg-Briand Pact. This was a promise not to go to war except for defense. However, hopeful agreements like this were not enough to stop the march toward war in the 1930s.

Bulgarian peasants selling wool at a street market in 1923. Close to 75 percent of Europeans still worked on the land in the 1920s.

War-Torn Europe

World War I caused heavy damage to Europe's fields and factories. There was a shortage of money to invest in new production. Recovery was slow, even in the Allied countries.

Germany was exhausted, and reparations payments made the situation worse. The new countries of central and eastern Europe also had difficulties. Prices rose, and millions of Europeans struggled to survive.

Prices rose, and millions of Europeans struggled to survive.

To protect their economies from outside competition, countries raised tariffs, or taxes on goods imported from other countries. Tariffs choked off free trade. Another of Wilson's Fourteen Points had failed.

America: The World's Powerhouse

Even before the end of World War I, the United States had risen above the European powers and become the most powerful country in the world. Britain still had a large empire, but the U.S. economy was far larger than any other.

With its great natural resources, factories, and financial power, the United States became the economic center of the world.

After the war, European countries became dependent on products from U.S. mines and factories. The countries of South America and Asia, which had formerly bought products from Europe, now shifted to buying U.S.-made goods.

As the United States became more involved in the world market, the country became even wealthier. With its great natural resources, factories, and financial power, the United States became the economic center of the world.

The U.S.S. *Jupiter* in dry dock in 1913. The United States was already the world's most powerful nation, but most Americans preferred to stay out of international affairs.

President Wilson meeting with his cabinet around 1920.

However, most Americans still preferred to stay out of world affairs. The United States had entered World War I reluctantly. Woodrow Wilson convinced people that the war was a moral crusade. He tried to make the Versailles peace conference the start of a new age of world peace, but he failed.

In the years that followed, Europe's old hatreds and rivalries resurfaced. Americans once again felt that they should keep to themselves and Europe should resolve its own conflicts. This policy is called isolationism. The U.S. Senate refused to ratify, or approve, the Treaty of Versailles. This was because the Senate did not want the U.S. to join the League of Nations.

In the years that followed, Europe's old hatreds and rivalries resurfaced.

In 1920 Warren Harding, an isolationist, succeeded President Wilson. As a result of Harding's policies, the U.S. did not participate in international peacekeeping efforts.

The New Nations of Eastern Europe

From 1282 to 1918, the Hapsburg dynasty dominated central Europe. They ruled the Holy Roman Empire and then the Austro-Hungarian Empire.

Austria became a democratic republic, but right-wing politicians began to rise to power. Their efforts prepared the way for a Nazi takeover.

In 1918 the last Hapsburg emperor gave up the throne. Austria and Hungary became separate countries. Austria had a population of barely six million. Most Austrians spoke German and wanted to unite with Germany. The Treaty of Versailles did not allow this. Austria became a democratic republic, but right-wing politicians began to rise to power. Their efforts prepared the way for a Nazi takeover.

Hungary became another small country, defeated and confused. A civil war broke out, eventually leading to a right-wing dictatorship. Hungary would later fight on the side of Nazi Germany.

Hungarian dictator Admiral Miklos Hrothy (*second from right*) and Hitler's deputy, Rudolf Hess, inspect German troops. Hrothy vowed vengeance on the Allied powers that had taken much of Hungary's territory.

POLAND AND THE TREATY OF RIGA

After World War I, Poland emerged as an independent country for the first time since the late 1700s.

The Poles were traditionally anti-Russian. In 1919 they were also deeply anti-communist. At the peace conference in Paris, the British foreign secretary, Lord Curzon, drew the Russian-Polish border. The border became known as the Curzon Line.

The Curzon Line left Russia with a large area of land that had once been part of Poland. Poland claimed the right to this land and attacked Russia in early 1920. The Russians pushed back and counter-attacked, advancing as far as the Polish capital, Warsaw. The Poles then beat back the Red Army troops.

The war ended in 1921 with the Treaty of Riga. Poland's border expanded beyond the Curzon Line to the east. The countries of western Europe, fearful of Communism, were relieved that the war was over.

Two new countries were created from lands of the Austro-Hungarian Empire: Czechoslovakia and Yugoslavia. Romania, formerly part of the Ottoman Empire, doubled in size by adding land from its neighbors, especially Russia.

Poland also reappeared on the map of Europe. The Polish people had been divided and ruled by foreign countries for many decades. The new Poland was larger, but included large numbers of non-Polish people.

National self-determination was a popular idea that turned out to be impossible in practice. Redrawing boundaries along purely cultural or ethnic lines always seemed to leave minorities of different cultures within each country. Most significantly, the new countries of Europe contained large numbers of German-speaking people.

National self-determination was a popular idea that turned out to be impossible in practice.

These new countries were small and weak, and their democratic governments were even weaker. This helped set the stage for future war.

Greek volunteers defending the frontier in Thessaly, Greece.

Turkey and Greece

At the end of World War I, the Ottoman Empire collapsed. The Allies imposed a peace treaty on Turkey in 1920. This treaty was called the Treaty of Sevres. The treaty broke apart the Ottoman Empire. Most of the Ottoman territories in Europe became independent countries. Ottoman lands in the Middle East became mandates under French and British control. The lands that remained formed the country of Turkey. It was limited to Asia Minor and the capital city of Constantinople, which lay in Europe. The lands of Asia Minor were rugged and economically backward. Trouble continued as Greece attacked Turkey.

In 1922 Turkey overthrew its sultanate, the old imperial form of government. A republic was formed in its place. The first president was an army officer, Mustafa Kemal (later called Kemal Atatürk, meaning Father of the Turks). He set out to turn Turkey into a modern country, modeled after Europe. Kemal abolished Islam as the national religion, granted equal rights to women, and built up industry. However, Kemal was not interested in democracy. He ruled Turkey as a dictatorship.

Greece won its independence from the Ottoman Empire in 1829. During World War I, Greece joined the Allied side As a result, Greece gained territory from Bulgaria and Turkey at the end of the war. Still, many ethnic Greeks lived in Asia Minor. This led Greece to invade Turkey in 1921. Turkey managed to defeat the invasion. Then, under the League of Nations, 1.5 million Greeks were moved from Asia Minor to Greece. At the same time, 800,000 Turks were transferred from Greece to Turkey. This helped to bring peace between the two countries.

THE WASHINGTON CONFERENCE, 1921 to 1922

KEY EVENTS

The Washington Conference met in late 1921. Representatives from nine nations met in Washington, D.C., to discuss future relations in East Asia. An important issue was the question of naval strength. After industrializing rapidly, Japan had the world's third-largest navy by then. Britain and the United States wanted to avoid an expensive arms race.

The key outcome of the conference was a treaty between Britain, France, Italy, the United States, and Japan. These countries agreed to limit the size of their navies. They promised not to build any new battleships or battlecruisers over the next ten years.

The treaty allowed Italy and France to have fewer battleships than Japan. This was a small indication of how world power was shifting away from Europe.

The Balkans

Many different groups demanded the right to self-determination.

The conflict between Turkey and Greece showed how difficult it was to make national boundaries. The mix of "nationalities" was the most complicated in the Balkans. The Balkans, the southeast corner of Europe, was a patchwork of cultures, religions, and languages. Many different groups demanded the right to self-determination. It was the Allied powers who ended up deciding who would receive that right.

Bulgaria, which had fought on the German side, lost territory. Serbia had fought on the Allied side and gained territory under the new name of Yugoslavia. The unequal treatment left bad feelings between these two rival countries.

A troublesome issue in the Balkans was the future of Macedonia. The region of Macedonia was divided between Greece and Yugoslavia. There were also a large number of ethnic Macedonians living in Bulgaria. Some of these armed themselves and carried out raids into Greece and Yugoslavia in 1924 and 1925. The Macedonian question remained unresolved. It stood out as an example of how stability would be hard to achieve in the Balkans.

Europe's Colonies

The Treaty of Versailles took away Germany's colonies.

Before World War I began, the British, French, and Dutch had large colonial empires. These empires survived World War I intact. However, nationalist feelings were growing around the world. In places such as India, more and more people wanted independence.

The Treaty of Versailles took away Germany's colonies. These colonies, in Africa and the Pacific, were given to the Allied powers. Most went to Britain; some went to France and Belgium. Germany's island colonies in the Pacific went to Japan. The Allies did not offer any colony the chance to rule itself.

Japan

World War I sparked massive industrial growth in Japan. Japan had wisely entered the war on the side of Britain and France. This let Japanese companies profit from building weapons and war supplies for the Allies. The Japanese built many new factories between 1914 and 1919.

Industrialization helped Japanese companies increase their exports of goods to Asian markets. The European powers were concentrating on other areas. Japan also gained a foothold in China. At the end of World War I, Japan seized Germany's territory in the province of Shantung. The Treaty of Versailles then awarded that territory to Japan. This decision greatly offended China and encouraged future aggression by Japan.

Japan also gained German island colonies in the Pacific. With Russia distracted by civil war, Japan became the strongest power in East Asia. The government in Tokyo wanted to expand even more.

However, the former German colonies were not just handed to new imperial rulers. They became mandates. The League of Nations created a commission, or committee, to check on the progress of the mandated territories. The ruling imperial powers were supposed to prepare the colonies for eventual independence.

Japan's industrial strength grew rapidly after World War I, helping to make it the strongest power in East Asia.

▶In 1923 Berlin, street protests erupted over high unemployment. Here, police are arresting several who have been involved in the disturbances and putting them into the patrol wagon.

2 Europe in the 1920s

When the Great War ended, most people felt the world had entered a new era. The 1920s brought many changes in culture, technology, and politics. There was hope that the world could be prosperous and peaceful again. Yet the decade of the 1920s ended with dark clouds hanging over Europe—the clouds of economic depression and totalitarianism on the rise.

Searching for National Security

In the aftermath of World War I, the victorious Allied countries still had one major worry: Germany. It seemed to them that Germany might still be a threat to peace. France, in particular, was frightened of Germany regaining its strength. The Treaty of Versailles aimed to keep Germany weak. There was a problem, though. Germany could simply disobey the treaty. They could refuse to pay reparations. They could rearm.

It seemed that France and Britain might be forced to go to war to enforce the treaty. Their weary people had no desire for another war. At the same time, Germany's reparations debt and the loss of the industrial region of the Saar weakened the democratic government. If Germany's democratic parties collapsed, extremists of the right wing would be in position to take over.

It seemed that France and Britain might be forced to go to war to enforce the treaty.

Despite Germany's default on reparations payments, there was some hope. Germany joined the League of Nations in 1926. In 1928, sixty-five countries signed the Kellogg-Briand Pact. These countries included the United States, Russia, and Germany. This treaty was a promise not to go to war except in self-defense.

In fact, the real danger to peace lay in eastern Europe. The collapse of the Austro-Hungarian Empire created confusion. Poland and Czechoslovakia lay between Germany and Russia. It was hoped that Poland would be a buffer between Germany and Russia. The weakness of these new countries created the possibility that Germany might expand eastward. To guard against this, France made more alliances with Poland, Czechoslovakia, Romania, and Yugoslavia.

Rebuilding France

The fighting of World War I took a heavy toll on France. The early 1920s brought an unstable economy and high inflation. However, conditions were not nearly as bad as those in Germany. The French economy began to recover. Gaining two industrial provinces, Alsace and Lorraine, provided a boost. These areas had been lost to Germany in a previous war, and returned to France in the Treaty of Versailles. By 1927, industrial production was back to pre-war levels, and it continued to grow rapidly.

Politics in France proved to be relatively stable. The Communist Party was strong enough to split, and therefore weaken, the left-wing forces of politics. But the Communists were not strong enough to make any major gains. The French parliament remained in the hands of moderately conservative parties. While the idea of democratic government was weakening in Germany, Italy, and Spain during this period, in France it remained strong.

The fighting of World War I took a heavy toll on France. The early 1920s brought an unstable economy and high inflation.

During World War I villages such as this one near Belleau Woods, France, were nearly destroyed.

Britain: A Declining Power

Britain took heavy losses among the country's young men during World War I. However, there had been very little physical damage to Britain itself. A large number of British merchant ships were sunk during the war. But these had been mostly replaced by 1918.

The war had a big impact on Britain's wealth. At the end of the war Britain owed about $3.8 billion to the United States. Many other European countries owed even more money to Britain. However, those countries were too poor to pay their debts.

Britain also suffered from a housing shortage and high unemployment after the war. New laws provided help to laid-off workers. Another new law gave the right to vote to all men over the age of twenty-one and to all women over the age of thirty.

Britain's Conservative Party held power for most of the 1920s. British workers staged some major strikes during this period. However, the Conservative government passed new laws that weakened the power of labor unions.

In 1918 U.S. president Woodrow Wilson had announced his Fourteen Points. One of his ideas was that all people had the right to self-determination. The age of colonial empires seemed to be drawing to an end. But the British Empire was still large and powerful.

Nevertheless, many parts of that empire (Canada, South Africa, Australia, and New Zealand) were moving toward full independence. They joined the League of Nations and increasingly saw themselves as countries, not colonies. Yet they still had deep connections to Britain.

Communist Russia

Revolution in 1917 ended the Russian monarchy. The czar, Nicholas II, abdicated, or gave up, the throne. A temporary government took over. But this government was unable to deal with the two biggest emergencies facing Russia: the war with Germany and the terrible poverty of the Russian peasants.

Throughout the country, soldiers, workers, and peasants formed soviets, or local governments. These groups stirred up more and more unrest. In November 1917, Vladimir Lenin and his Bolsheviks, one wing of the Communist Party, overthrew the temporary government.

In 1918 Russian revolutionary leader Vladimir Ilich Lenin split with the Left Social Revolutionaries and renamed the Bolsheviks the Russian Communist Party.

Lenin made peace with Germany. He also allowed the peasants to take over the lands of their landlords. Still, Lenin did not have the support of the majority of the people. But Lenin was no democrat. He used his secret police, the Cheka, to murder thousands of people who opposed him. Civil war raged for three years between the Bolsheviks and anticommunists, known as the Whites.

By 1921 Russia was exhausted and bankrupt. Several million people had died of famine. Lenin had placed the entire economy of the country under government control. When the civil war ended, he allowed some private businesses and open markets. This was successful, and by 1928 Russian production had returned to 1914 levels.

Lenin died in 1924. This led to a power struggle in the Communist Party. Leon Trotsky argued that Russia should use its resources to spread revolution. On the other hand, Joseph Stalin wanted to concentrate on the welfare of the country. Eventually, Trotsky was exiled from Russia in 1929. Joseph Stalin became the absolute ruler of Russia, which by then was called the Union of Soviet Socialist Republics (USSR).

Communism and the Democracies

When the Bolsheviks took power in Russia, the Western democracies decided to respond.

When the Bolsheviks took power in Russia, the Western democracies decided to respond. They feared that Communism would spread through Europe, so they sent troops to help the people who were fighting the Communists. These people were called the Whites. The Bolsheviks, or Communists, were known as the Reds.

Britain sent troops and tanks to fight the Bolsheviks. But British public opinion turned against the operation. British forces withdrew in late 1919. France sent support to Poland, which was at war with Soviet forces.

Although the Communists finally won control of the Soviet Union, the country was badly battered. The ideal of Communism was to spread revolution throughout the world. But during the 1920s, the Soviets were mostly occupied with the situation inside their own country.

JOSEPH STALIN

KEY FIGURES

Joseph Stalin (1879–1953) was born Iosif Djusgashvili in the country of Georgia. This mountainous country is located south of what is now Russia. Djusgashvili later took the name Stalin, meaning "man of steel." As a young man he became involved in revolutionary politics. In 1903, he became a follower of Vladimir Lenin, leader of the Bolsheviks.

Imperial Russian police twice sent Stalin to Siberia for his revolutionary views. Each time he escaped. He was also imprisoned from 1913 to 1916. In 1917 he became editor of *Pravda*, the Bolshevik newspaper. Stalin was not an intellectual or a gifted speaker. He was, however, a clever political operator. By staying in the background and making few enemies, Stalin quickly rose through the party ranks.

During the civil war he was noted for bravery in the Battle of Tsaritsyn (later called Stalingrad). After the war, he quietly built up a network of friends in important offices. After Lenin died, Stalin used this network to grab power. Once in control, he dealt with his rivals ruthlessly. He was the leader of the Soviet Union until his death in 1953.

Joseph Stalin

Fascism in Italy

Unlike Russia and Germany, Italy still had a constitutional monarchy at the end of World War I. A king and a parliament shared power. This system proved to be fragile, however. Italy was one of the victorious Allied powers. But it played only a small role in the postwar peacemaking. Some Italians were angry that the Allies had not given Italy the town of Fiume. This town in Yugoslavia had a majority of Italian-speaking citizens.

Italy was not as strong as France or Britain in natural resources or factories. In the early 1920s, prices rose sharply and unemployment was high. Rampant crime in the south and raging industrial strikes in the north created a feeling of crisis. The right-wing Fascist Party, founded by Benito Mussolini, grew rapidly. Their main positions were opposition to socialism and a call for strong government authority. The party took its name from the *fasces* of ancient Rome. The fasces were a symbol stood for the strength of the Roman Empire. The message was that Fascists would return Italy to a place of glory in the world.

Italy was not as strong as France or Britain in natural resources or factories. In the early 1920s, prices rose sharply and unemployment was high.

In the elections of 1921, the Fascists played on popular fear of Communism. They won thirty-five seats in the Italian parliament. In a speech, Mussolini declared he was proud to be the enemy of democracy. In the summer of 1922, gangs of Fascists roamed the streets. They attacked socialists and took control in several towns. The liberal prime minister resigned. Italy seemed to be on the brink of civil war.

The king of Italy, Victor Emmanuel III, wanted to end the crisis. He decided to support Mussolini.

Mussolini announced that he and his followers would make a "March on Rome." The king of Italy, Victor Emmanuel III, wanted to end the crisis. He decided to support Mussolini. The king invited Mussolini to become prime minister.

Parliament voted to give Mussolini special dictatorial powers for one year. This was long enough for the Fascists to take permanent control of the government. The Fascist dictatorship stayed in place until 1945.

Germany's Weimar Republic

Defeat in World War I left Germany in chaos. The emperor, Kaiser Wilhelm II, gave up the throne. The government changed from a monarchy to a republic. The government was called the Weimar Republic, after the town where an assembly wrote the constitution. The Weimar Republic faced many threats. In the early 1920s there were several uprisings by Communists and right-wing groups. One of these was Adolf Hitler's Munich Putsch, an attempt to gain power by force, in 1923.

The greatest danger to stability was the economy. Germany's economy was crippled. Inflation ran out of control. In late 1921 one U.S. dollar was equal to 162 German marks. By November 1923 it took 4.2 million German marks to buy one dollar. It took a suitcase full of notes to buy a pint of milk. Businesses collapsed. Thousands of workers lost their jobs. Many others went on strike. Inflation wiped out the life savings of middle-class people.

BENITO MUSSOLINI

KEY FIGURES

Benito Mussolini (1883–1945) was dictator of Italy from 1922 to 1945. Like Germany's Adolf Hitler, he was known for his dramatic speeches.

At a young age he was expelled from school for stabbing a fellow student. He worked various jobs, eventually joining the Socialist Party and working as a left-wing journalist.

Mussolini was wounded in battle during his service in World War I. The experience changed him into a conservative nationalist. He began to work with radical nationalist groups. One of these was the Fascio di Combattimento, or the Fascists. Mussolini rose to be leader of this group. In his speeches Mussolini openly called for violence. "It is blood," he declared, "which moves the wheels of history."

In November 1921 he declared himself *Il Duce* (leader) of the Fascists. Within a year he was made prime minister, in fact dictator, of Italy.

Benito Mussolini (*right*) addressing a crowd.

The Stresemann Years

At the peak of the economic crisis in 1923, a new chancellor, Gustav Stresemann, came into office. He realized that economic recovery was needed to save Germany's democracy. He ended major strikes by factory workers. He introduced a new German mark, replacing the old, worthless money. He also promised the Allies that Germany would pay reparations.

Stresemann was chancellor for just a few months.

The governments of Britain and the United States rewarded Stresemann's efforts. They created the Dawes Plan. This made generous loans to Germany, which helped rebuild her economy.

Stresemann was chancellor for just a few months. Then, for the rest of the decade, he was foreign secretary. Because he helped bring stability back to Germany, those years became known as the Stresemann years. In this time, Germany prospered. When Germany joined the League of Nations in 1926, it seemed to be a major step. Germany seemed to be rejoining the family of respected nations.

This is a map of Germany during the early years of the Weimar Republic. It shows the principal attempts to overthrow the government.

Hyperinflation ruined the Germany economy. By late November 1923, one U.S. dollar was equal to 1 trillion German marks. This woman is starting a morning fire with marks "not worth the paper they are printed on."

However, serious problems remained. Left-wing and right-wing political groups had their own private armies. They committed murders and fought each other in the streets. Of all these groups, the most dangerous was the National Socialist Party, led by Adolf Hitler.

After the war, Hitler attended right-wing political meetings. He discovered that he had a talent for public speaking. This, plus his ruthlessness and his unshakable belief in his own ideas, carried him to political leadership.

In prison after leading the Munich Putsch, Hitler wrote Mein Kampf.

In prison after leading the Munich Putsch, Hitler wrote *Mein Kampf (My Struggle)*. It was a mixture of autobiography and political musings. In it he lashes out against the Jews and demands that Germany rise to become a new empire: the Third German Reich.

ADOLF HITLER

Adolf Hitler

Adolf Hitler (1889–1945) was born in Braunau am Inn, Austria-Hungary. As a child he did not do well in school and had trouble making friends. In his teenage years he became very interested in the operas of Richard Wagner. These operas celebrated the past glories of Germanic culture.

Hitler's ambition was to be a painter. Twice the Vienna Academy of Fine Arts refused to accept him. Until 1914 he lived in Vienna, lonely and poor. These years shaped Hitler's personality. His dreams of artistic achievement were dashed and he was unable to settle into any trade or career.

As he later revealed in his autobiography *Mein Kampf* (*My Struggle*), Hitler blamed everyone but himself for his unsuccessful life. He came to despise Vienna and Vienna's middle class as well as Jews. Hitler wished to see his native Austria absorbed into Germany.

Hitler welcomed the outbreak of World War I. He served with distinction as a message runner in the German Army. Twice Hitler was awarded the Iron Cross for bravery. When Germany surrendered in 1918, Hitler felt sure the country had been betrayed by its political leaders.

The Nazis: From Street Fighting to Politics

The German Workers' Party was one of several left-wing groups formed after World War I. It had only a handful of members when Adolf Hitler attended one of its meetings in 1919. Unexpectedly, Hitler spoke up at the meeting. The group's leader was impressed and invited Hitler to join.

Within a little more than a year, Hitler had become leader of the party. He changed its name to the Nationalsozialistische Deutsche Arbeiterpartei (National Socialist German Workers' Party). It was also known as the Nazi Party. The name was designed to appeal to both right-wing nationalists and left-wing socialists.

Hitler's great skill was in public speaking. Within three years the party had grown from one hundred members to more than 5,000. Hitler established the Sturmabteilung (SA), or storm troopers. They were organized like a small army. They engaged in street fighting, especially against the Communists. Hitler also shaped the ideas and goals of the party.

Hitler claimed that Germany had been "stabbed in the back," and that Jews and Communists were destroying the country. He did not hide his hatred for democratic government. In 1923 he believed it was time for a putsch, or an attempt to seize power by force.

POLITICAL WORLD — THE TWENTY-FIVE POINTS

After the failure of the Munich Putsch, Hitler decided that the Nazis could only come to power by legal means. However, the Nazis remained antidemocratic and anti-Semitic, or anti-Jew.

The Twenty-five Points of the party's 1925 program are surprisingly honest. The Nazis demanded the union of all Germans in Austria and eastern Europe. This would form a "Great Germany" with much larger boundaries. They called for *lebensraum*, or living space, in the east. This would be land seized from other countries to allow the German population to grow.

Above all, Germany was to be only for people with "German blood." Jews would not be allowed. Finally, the Nazis demanded an end to democracy. They wanted to rule Germany as a dictatorship.

The result was the Munich Putsch. It was also called the Beer Hall Putsch because it began in a beer hall. The uprising lasted only one day. When police opened fire on the marching Nazis, the rebels gave up on the putsch.

Hitler himself was slightly wounded and was arrested. He was sent to prison, but the episode made him famous. For the first time millions of Germans heard about the Nazis and their ideas. They also heard Hitler's dramatic speech during his trial. He declared that he was not a criminal, but the savior of the nation. He said he would rescue Germany from the "real villains." Most understood him to mean the democratic government and the Jews.

Hitler served only eight months in prison. The whole affair made him famous. In prison he wrote his autobiography, *Mein Kampf (My Struggle)*. In it he spelled out his hatred for the Jews. He also stated that Germany needed to overthrow the Versailles settlement and conquer eastern Europe.

By the time Hitler was released from prison, the German economy was improving. The mood of the country was not right for an open attack on the Weimar Republic. Instead the Nazis continued to build up their fame.

Joseph Goebbels, Hitler's top assistant, perfected the use of propaganda. He organized a series of party rallies, held in Nuremberg. These rallies were highly elaborate. They featured massive crowds, flags and emblems, military-style uniforms, precise marching, and "Heil Hitler" salutes. These images were deeply appealing to the German people. Hitler's popularity grew.

The 1928 Elections and the Young Plan

The Nazis continued their street fighting. Goebbels said in 1927, "Whoever can conquer the street will one day conquer the state." The Nazis also remained openly opposed to democracy. They did not do well in the 1928 parliamentary elections. The Nazis won only 3 percent of the vote. This gave them only twelve seats in the parliament, or Reichstag. They ranked as the ninth political party in Germany.

Germany's main right-wing political party was the Nationalist Party. They were also the third-largest party. In the summer of 1929, however, the nationalists made a key error. They decided to campaign against the Young Plan for repayment of reparations. They invited Hitler to join their campaign.

The nationalists thought that Hitler's speaking abilities would increase their public support. In reality, the campaign waged against the Young Plan failed miserably. The German people supported the Young Plan by a wide margin. However, Hitler, by being invited to take part, became a part of the "respectable" right wing. He dominated the campaign. Day after day, his name and picture were on the front page of the newspaper. Support for the Nazis grew much greater. In 1929, Hitler and the Nazis were still a fairly small party. But the arrival of the Great Depression gave them another sharp boost and changed the course of German history.

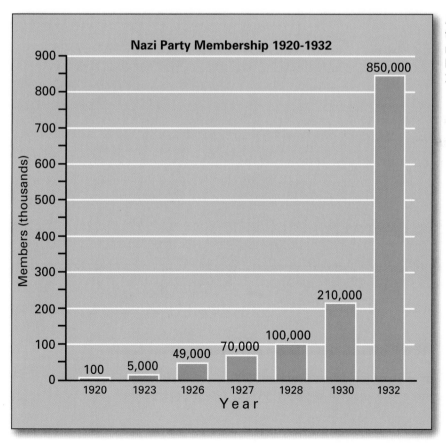

A chart showing the growth in the membership of the Nazi Party between 1920 and 1932.

Unemployed men waiting for a free lunch in 1931. The 1920s were a time of optimism and economic growth, but the Great Depression caused widespread suffering.

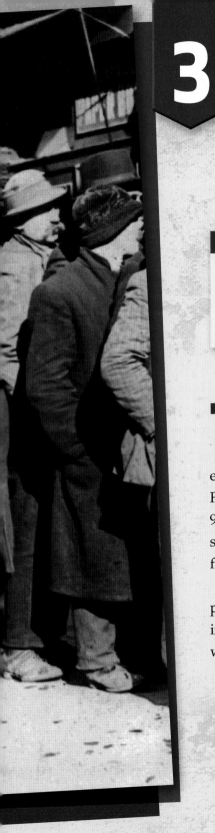

3 The United States Between the Wars

KEY PEOPLE	KEY PLACES
Calvin Coolidge	New York, New York
Herbert Hoover	San Francisco, California
Huey Long	Pueblo, Colorado
Franklin Roosevelt	Washington, D.C.

The United States emerged in a strong position after World War I. In two years of fighting during World War I, the United States suffered around 75,000 dead. Compared with other countries, U.S. losses were low. Russia lost 1.7 million people; France lost 1.36 million; Germany lost 1.8 million; and Britain lost 906,000. Unlike other countries in World War I, the United States suffered no physical damage from the fighting. The war's battlefields were in Europe, the Middle East, and Africa.

In economic terms, the war helped U.S. industry. Demand for products increased. Women and African Americans entered the industrial workforce. By the end of World War I, the United States was undoubtedly the world's economic superpower.

A Return to Isolationism

After World War I, most Americans wanted to return to the country's traditional policy, staying out of world affairs as much as possible. This policy was known as isolationism. On the other hand, President Woodrow Wilson wanted the United States to act as a leader in the world.

During World War I, Wilson tried to keep the United States neutral at first. Finally, German attacks on international shipping cost U.S. lives and damaged U.S. trade. When three U.S. ships were sunk in three days in March, 1916, Wilson asked Congress to declare war on Germany. The United States joined the war on the side of Britain and France against Germany and its allies.

Wilson was an idealist. He believed that the role of the United States was to help other nations solve their problems without warfare.

Wilson was an idealist. He believed that the role of the United States was to help other nations solve their problems without warfare. In 1918 he presented his Fourteen Points. The president believed they should form the basis of the peace. The points included open diplomacy and freedom of trade. They called for the adjustment of Europe's borders to give self-government to minority groups. Finally, they called for an association of nations that would solve disputes peacefully—a League of Nations. To the weary people of Europe, Wilson became a hero.

President Wilson's goals did not match those of his Allies (France, Britain, and Italy). The victorious Allies, in particular the French, wanted to punish Germany. The final peace agreement reflected the French viewpoint. Germany had to accept the blame for starting the war. They also had to pay huge fines, called reparations. In addition, Germany lost 12 percent of its land. The harshness of the treaty angered the German people. It helped bring Adolf Hitler to power.

Wilson had another shock when he returned home from Europe. The Republicans in Congress were strongly isolationist. In September 1919 the Senate refused to ratify the Versailles Peace Treaty. Many Americans did not want to be pulled into the conflicts of Europe. It seemed that joining the League of Nations could do just that.

Wilson fought hard for the treaty. In September 1919 he decided to go on a speaking tour to persuade people to support the treaty. Wilson traveled on a special train through the West, making forty speeches. Wilson reduced his audiences to tears with speeches about the threat of another war and about the sacrifice of the American war dead. The tour exhausted him. After a speech in Pueblo, Colorado, his health forced him to abandon the tour. In October he suffered a stroke. From then on, Wilson governed by using his wife to carry messages to his cabinet.

The United States would not join the League of Nations or ratify the Treaty of Versailles.

The Senate refused to ratify the treaty. The United States would not join the League of Nations or ratify the Treaty of Versailles. The country had turned its back on Europe.

The Business of America Is Business

Issues at home took the attention of the American people. Prices rose rapidly while wages stayed the same. Unemployment rose, bringing labor unrest. During 1919 about 4 million Americans went on strike. They called for higher pay or better working conditions. In Boston the police force went on strike. Coal miners and steelworkers walked out across the country. For many Americans, this unrest was too serious to be blamed on U.S.-born workers. They placed the blame on a new villain: Communism.

Issues at home took the attention of the American people.

Communist revolutionaries took control of Russia in 1917. Two years later Communists formed the Third International. The goal of this organization was to spread Communism around the world. The American Communist Party was formed in the United States in 1919. Most of its members were immigrant workers. A few members urged violence, and they were blamed for bomb attacks in eight U.S. cities. The federal government responded with the "red scare." A new section of the Department of Justice worked to root out radicals. This division later became the FBI. Between 5,000 and 10,000 people were rounded up and deported, most without a trial. The scare faded the following year.

In 1920 the presidential election pitted Republican Warren Harding against Democrat James Cox. Harding, a senator from Ohio, called for a return to "normalcy." Although he never stated exactly what he meant by normalcy, he won a landslide victory.

Harding was an isolationist. He placed limits on immigration.

Harding was an isolationist. He placed limits on immigration. He raised tariffs—taxes on imported products. Americans were in a mood to return to an imagined golden age of the past. The Ku Klux Klan reappeared and grew. The Ku Klux Klan used violence, including murder and beatings, against blacks, Jews, Catholics, and immigrants.

Prohibition was another attempt to return to "rural values." It became the law in 1919. This was a ban on the making and selling of liquor and beer. But an illegal network of liquor-sellers and bars soon sprang up. This network was dominated by gangsters, such as Al Capone.

While it seemed like the United States wanted to totally withdraw from world affairs, it was now too powerful and wealthy to stay uninvolved. U.S. troops intervened in Nicaragua, Honduras, and Haiti to protect American business interests. Meanwhile, Americans watched uneasily as extremism grew in Europe. Armed Communists and Fascists fought in the streets in Germany. Benito Mussolini came to power in Italy.

President Harding died in office in August 1923. His vice president, Calvin Coolidge, became president. Coolidge easily won the 1924 election. A strong supporter of business, he famously said, "The business of America is business." As president, Coolidge tried to reduce government interference in the economy.

America's economy grew rapidly during Coolidge's presidency. The stock market rose higher and higher. There were some warning signs of trouble ahead. But Americans spent their money freely, assuming the good times would go on forever. Banks made loans easier to get. Consumer debt rose sharply. It became very popular to borrow money to buy stocks.

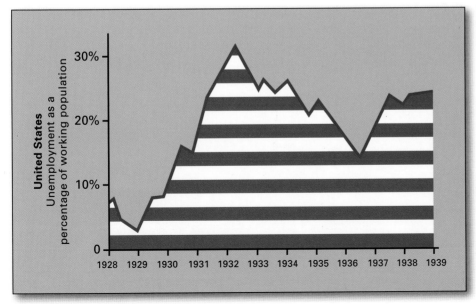

There was a steep rise in unemployment between 1928 and 1939.

From Boom to Bust

In 1927, President Coolidge decided not to run for reelection. The Secretary of Commerce, Herbert Hoover, became the Republican nominee. He easily won the 1928 election against Alfred E. Smith. Unfortunately, Hoover would become forever associated with the worst depression in U.S. history. Surprisingly, his experience seemed to prepare him well for the presidency. Hoover made a fortune in mining and railroad construction. From the moment Hoover entered public service in 1914, he never took any pay. He gave all his salary to charity.

Hoover became famous during World War I. He was the head of a commission trying to help starving citizens of Belgium. Later he also sent food aid to Russia, which was hit by famine after the Communist revolution in 1917. Hoover had a solid reputation. When he was sworn in, the prospects for the country seemed good.

Six months later, on October 24, 1929, "Black Thursday," there was a steep drop in stock prices. Panicked investors sold off millions of shares. The market stabilized by the end of the day, and the weekend was quiet.

A nervous crowd gathers on Wall Street on "Black Thursday," October 24, 1929. The stock market crash was the biggest in history, wiping $28 billion from share prices and ushering in the Great Depression.

Black Tuesday

On Monday, October 28, the downward slide continued. The next day, Black Tuesday, brought the final crash. The stock market lost an estimated $10 billion in value. This was probably twice the amount of currency in circulation in the country at the time. Price continued to fall for three weeks after Black Tuesday. The stock market crash then spread to the banking sector.

The Great Depression

The Wall Street crash had a deep effect on the American people. The optimism of the 1920s was shattered. However, the crash was not the only cause of the Great Depression, although it contributed to it. One cause was the cycle of economic expansions and contractions, or boom and bust. The prosperity of the 1920s would be inevitably be followed by slower growth or decline. But the decline of the Great Depression was much more severe than any before.

Another cause of the Depression, which spread around the world, lay in U.S. trade policy. Hoover had wanted to help U.S. farmers. He tried to get Congress to raise tariffs on imported farm products. His proposal helped cause a general raising of tariffs on not only agricultural produce, but manufactured goods, too.

POLITICAL WORLD · THE BONUS MARCHERS

In summer 1932 a group of around 10,000 World War I veterans and their families marched on Washington, D.C. They called themselves the Bonus Army. Most of them had been out of work since the beginning of the Great Depression. They were protesting not receiving bonus payments for their military services. They set up a shantytown—a settlement of makeshift huts—and marched in front of the U.S. Capitol building daily.

President Hoover insisted that the country could not afford to pay the veterans. Then he ordered police and troops to remove the marchers peacefully. The military commander, General Douglas MacArthur, thought the marchers were nothing but troublemakers and Communists. On his orders, troops attacked the protesters and burned down the shantytown. Several veterans were killed and hundreds were injured. Two babies died in the fire.

As the United States put high tariffs in place, European countries reacted by raising their own tariffs. These moves choked world trade. This made the Depression deeper and longer.

Across America the downturn took its toll. Personal incomes dropped. Unemployment rose rapidly, from around 3 percent to 25 percent of the workforce. Many businesses closed. At the same time, a million farmers in the Great Plains suffered from a severe drought.

Hoover believed the government should not interfere with the economy. He refused to send government money to help the jobless and hungry. Around the country many of these needy people built communities of shacks. These shantytowns ironically became known as Hoovervilles.

The president still believed that the crisis would pass. But the crisis only got worse in 1931. In 1932 he decided the government had to get

Shantytown communities sprang up overnight. They were sometimes called "Hoovervilles." Many people blamed President Hoover for letting the nation slide into depression.

ALEC WILDER

Alec Wilder was a young man living in New York City in the 1920s. In 1929 the banker's son became aware that everyone around him, even hotel bell-boys, were using any money they could get their hands on to buy stocks on margin. Increasingly anxious that the stock market was heading for disaster, Wilder went to see his family's financial adviser.

I talked to this charming man and told him I wanted to unload this stock. Just because I had this feeling of disaster. He got very sentimental: "Oh, your father wouldn't have liked you to do that." He was so persuasive, I said OK. I could have sold it for $160,000. Six weeks later, the Crash. Four years later, I sold it for $4,000.

I wasn't mad at him, strangely enough. But I wanted nothing to do with money. The blow had fallen, and it was over. I was very skeptical and never invested. I became tired of people telling me: "Oh, there's this marvelous thing happening, and if you should have any extra money…" I'd say, "Don't talk to me about the market." I'd have nothing to do with it.

—Quoted in *Hard Times* by Studs Terkel

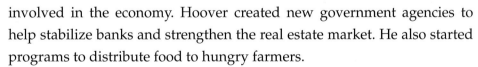

involved in the economy. Hoover created new government agencies to help stabilize banks and strengthen the real estate market. He also started programs to distribute food to hungry farmers.

The government also started a number of public works projects. Public works projects often construct or improve structures like roads, bridges, and government buildings. They also serve to create jobs.

Hoover's measures were later echoed by his successor, Franklin D. Roosevelt. But for many Americans, Hoover's efforts were too little, too late. He was seen as not caring about the people hurt by the Depression.

Roosevelt and the New Deal

Franklin D. Roosevelt came from a wealthy New York family. He was a distant cousin of former U.S. president Theodore Roosevelt. Roosevelt served as a senator in New York. He gained fame for fighting corruption.

Roosevelt's wife, Eleanor, was a highly gifted organizer and leader. She was a fighter for human rights. Although their marriage was troubled, they stayed together. Each saw in the other an essential ally for achieving their respective political and social goals.

Roosevelt served as assistant secretary of the Navy under Woodrow Wilson. He then ran, unsuccessfully, as the Democratic Party's vice-presidential candidate in 1920. Then, in 1921, Roosevelt contracted polio. The disease left his legs paralyzed. But he carefully projected a public image of strength and energy. He kept up the appearance of walking by using crutches and leg braces.

Farmers in the 1930s suffered from a severe drought. Herbert Hoover did not seem to care about hardships like these, so voters elected Franklin D. Roosevelt as president in 1932.

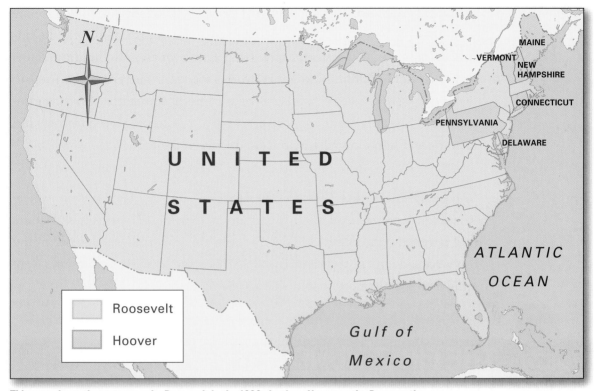

This map shows the states won by Roosevelt in the 1932 election. He ran as the Democratic candidate against Hoover.

Roosevelt returned to politics and served as governor of New York. At the start of the Great Depression, he began the country's first system of government relief to unemployed people. These programs made him the ideal Democratic candidate for the presidential election of 1932.

Roosevelt promised to tackle the economic crisis. He called for greater government control over utilities, for tax breaks for farmers, and for federal unemployment relief. These measures went against an American tradition of self-reliance and limited government. But his ideas attracted public support. Roosevelt won a strong majority over Hoover.

Roosevelt started his presidency with a flurry of laws and directives. This period was called the First Hundred Days. He called his program the New Deal. He pushed through a law to stabilize banks. He made the first of his radio broadcasts. These were known as Fireside Chats. He reassured the public that he was working to solve the problems they faced.

Roosevelt started his presidency with a flurry of laws and directives.

Other major new programs followed. Some established public works projects. These included reforesting rural areas and building dams to generate electricity. Other programs tried to increase the income of farmers by limiting production. Other programs provided assistance to unemployed people and farmers and home owners who were deeply in debt.

Opposition to the New Deal

Roosevelt's programs earned him many enemies among business leaders and political conservatives. They thought the government was becoming too involved with economic activity. To them, the New Deal programs were similar to socialism, or worse, Communism.

THE FIRST HUNDRED DAYS

KEY EVENTS

The period from March 9 to June 16, 1933, produced many new programs. These are the new laws that Roosevelt asked Congress to pass to make the New Deal a reality during the early days of his administration:

March 9 Emergency Banking Relief Act
March 20 Economy Act
March 22 Beer-Wine Revenue Act
March 31 Civilian Conservation Corps, Reforestation Relief Act
May 12 Federal Emergency Relief Act
May 12 Agricultural Adjustment Administration
May 18 Tennessee Valley Authority
May 25 Federal Securities Act
June 5 Gold Repeal Joint Resolution
June 6 National Employment System Act
June 13 Home Owners Refinancing Act
June 16 Banking Act
June 16 Farm Credit Act
June 16 Emergency Railroad Transportation Act
June 16 National Industrial Recovery Act

LABOR CONFLICTS

During the Depression, labor unions became more powerful. Poverty and harsh economic conditions drove more and more workers to join unions. Large unions had the ability to shut down important industries.

Strikes often led to violence. Employers would try to hire scabs, or unofficial workers. They might also bring in hired thugs, known as goons, to frighten workers. The police also often used violence to break up strikes.

In 1934 there were strikes in the Kentucky coal mines. There was also a general strike in San Francisco. Both strikes were met with violence.

In 1937 more than a dozen people were shot in during a strike at Ford Motor Company. Henry Ford was bitterly opposed to unionization. So he hired 800 goons and paid more than 9,000 employees to inform on their fellow workers' political activities.

Some of the most important challenges to Roosevelt's New Deal came from the U.S. Supreme Court. The court declared that six key acts were unconstitutional. They decided these programs infringed on the rights of individuals, companies, or states.

There were other critics. Huey Long served as the governor of Louisiana, and later a U.S. senator. He demanded a much more radical program of economic reform. Another voice of criticism was Father Charles Coughlin, a radical Catholic priest. He used radio broadcasts to win public support for his ideas.

Some of the most important challenges to Roosevelt's New Deal came from the U. S. Supreme Court.

Coughlin called for a mass nationalization of U.S. banks, utilities, and natural resources. Later, when he began to speak admiringly of Adolf Hitler and Benito Mussolini, it cost him much of his public support.

Huey Long and Father Coughlin started the Union Party and planned to run their own candidate in the 1936 election. However, Long was assassinated, cutting the effort short.

Roosevelt's other enemies included labor unions. The unions felt that he had not gone far enough to support them. Many Democrats from the far right and left wings of the party also criticized Roosevelt. Still, Roosevelt remained very popular.

Roosevelt decided to take a cross-country trip by rail. He wanted to create the widest possible coalition of voters.

The Republican candidate was a moderate, Alf Landon. But his running mate, Frank Knox, was not. Knox's extreme views alienated many moderate voters. Meanwhile, Roosevelt decided to take a cross-country trip by rail. He wanted to create the widest possible coalition of voters. And his efforts paid off. Roosevelt easily won reelection in 1936 by the largest margin in more than a hundred years.

President Roosevelt campaigning by rail in 1936. He went on to win the election by the largest majority vote in the last century.

THE WORKS PROGRESS ADMINISTRATION (WPA)

The Works Progress Administration was Roosevelt's major agency for reducing unemployment. The WPA created jobs by building schools, bridges, roads, and other structures. It employed 3 million people at a cost of $11 billion. The WPA changed the face of the nation with the work on new or repaired roads, public buildings, dams, and hospitals.

The WPA also employed artists, actors, writers, and musicians. They left a great legacy of public art. Another project of the WPA was the study and preservation of American folk art traditions.

He won nearly 28 million votes, nearly 12 million more than the Republican candidate. In the electoral college, Roosevelt's win was even more impressive: 523 to 8.

In his inaugural speech in 1937, Roosevelt outlined the problems the country still faced. He said, "I see one-third of a nation ill-housed, ill-clad and ill-nourished."

Still, in Roosevelt's second term, the momentum of the New Deal started to run out. Many Republicans and Democrats alike felt that Roosevelt was trying to dominate all branches of the U.S. government. Many of his proposals in his second term were not passed, or were limited. One of his last major New Deal laws was the Fair Labor Standards Act. Passed in June 1938,

In Roosevelt's second term, the momentum of the New Deal started to run out.

it abolished child labor in many industries. It also introduced the regulation of hours and pay to others. As he put down his pen after signing the legislation, he said: "That's that."

▶**A procession of Nazis carrying standards inspired by the Roman Empire.** The Nazis held party rallies like this one to create a powerful and appealing image of triumph and strength.

4 Building Nazi Germany

KEY PEOPLE	KEY PLACES
⚑ Herman Göring	⚑ Berlin, Germany
⚑ Heinrich Himmler	⚑ Rhineland, Germany
⚑ Paul von Hindenburg	⚑ Sudetenland, Czechoslovakia
⚑ Adolf Hitler	⚑ Vienna, Austria
⚑ Ernst Röhm	

I n the late 1920s, Adolf Hitler and his party, the National Socialist Workers Party (NSDP) or Nazis, were a minor party in Germany. They were primarily known for staging a failed coup called the Munich Putsch in 1923. But membership in the Nazi Party grew over the decade. In 1930, they won 6 million votes and 107 seats in parliament. Three years later, Hitler became chancellor of Germany. The crucial question is how this happened.

Germany's Economic Collapse

In the late 1920s, radical parties like the Nazis were not very popular in Germany. This changed when the Great Depression began. This economic crisis pushed political systems in many countries, including Germany, to the breaking point.

These stamps were offered and sold in Germany by the Communist Party before the 1932 election. They depict the Red Army.

The Great Depression was much worse in Germany than in the United States. The Treaty of Versailles imposed responsibility for World War I on Germany as well as the burden of reparations payments to the Allies. To make the payments, the German government printed more paper money. Eventually, this led to runaway inflation, or hyperinflation, in 1923 and 1924. Hyperinflation destroyed savings and investments and ruined the German middle class. This led to widespread anger and disillusionment with democracy. Some Germans also felt victimized by the Treaty of Versailles. They were among the first to notice the appeal of Hitler and the Nazi Party.

By the late 1920s, Weimar Germany seemed to be doing well. Paul von Hindenburg, a popular hero of World War I, served as president of the republic, giving a sense of stability. Loans from the United States boosted the economy. However, the situation was worse than it seemed. The banking system depended on the U.S. loans. If those loans dried up, the whole German economy would be in deep trouble.

Another weakness was the farming sector. It was depressed even before the Wall Street Crash of 1929. Many farmers went bankrupt, and the government made no effort to help them. The Nazis took advantage of this. In the elections of 1928, the Nazis gained support in rural areas. In December there were almost 2 million unemployed people in Germany. They were another group that was willing to listen to Hitler.

In 1931 the country's economic problems spread to the banks. In July a leading German bank went bankrupt. People all over Germany rushed to get their money out of their bank accounts. This caused the whole banking system to collapse. The rest of the economy collapsed soon after. Germany's Gross National Product, the sum of all goods and services produced in the country, fell by almost half. The number of unemployed almost tripled. By late 1932, 5.6 million Germans were unemployed.

Many farmers went bankrupt, and the government made no effort to help them.

The 1930 Election

Germany's political system was paralyzed by the economic disaster. The government made almost no moves to stop the emergency. Extremist parties—the German Communist Party and the Nazis—stood to benefit from the situation. Hitler saw that this was his chance to make his party a national political force.

In the election of 1930, the Nazis won 18.3 percent of the vote. They became the second-largest party in the Reichstag. Now they had a serious chance to gain power.

At the same time, this success created a new problem. Hitler needed to act like a respectable party leader. He had no choice but to restrain the Nazi thugs of the *Sturmabteilung* or the SA. These men, also called storm troopers, were led by a tough war veteran, Captain Ernst Röhm. Hitler temporarily banned them from their political street fights in 1931. This created a split within the Nazi Party.

Hitler Demands Power

As the leader of a major political party, Hitler was now an important figure. He began to associate with Germany's political, economic, and military leaders. Mainstream political leaders had mixed reactions to Hitler. Some conservatives saw him as an ally to help them balance the Communists. Others saw him as a threat to democracy and refused to deal with him.

Hindenburg thought that Hitler was unsuited to be chancellor. At best, he thought, Hitler might become a minister.

In October 1931, German president Paul von Hindenburg invited Hitler to meet. However, the former general was unimpressed with Hitler. Hindenburg thought that Hitler was unsuited to be chancellor. At best, he thought, Hitler might become a minister.

Hitler was not upset by Hindenburg's reaction. One week later, at a rally of 100,000 SA troops, Hitler predicted the Nazis would seize power the following year.

KEY EVENTS

The Nazis understood the value of spectacular displays. The annual party rallies at Nuremberg Stadium were the most impressive expression of pomp and pageantry. The stadium filled with tens of thousands of eager party supporters, all dressed in uniform.

To heighten the excitement, Hitler always arrived late. Music blared from hundreds of loudspeakers around the arena. The crowd sang the Nazi hymn or the German national anthem. Finally Hitler would enter the stadium as the crowd thundered.

Hitler would make his way to the podium and begin to give his speech. He would slowly warm up, gradually raising his voice. The crowd would interrupt him with applause and shouts of "Heil Hitler." Even outside observers such as U.S. journalists agreed that the experience was intense.

The 1932 Election

Hitler realized that the Nazi Party would need allies to win control of the German government. He set out to make partnerships with the Nationalist Party and other German conservatives. Hitler believed he could turn these partnerships to his own advantage.

Hitler realized that the Nazi Party would need allies to win control of the German government.

Germany's government was led by a chancellor, or prime minister, and a president. President Hindenburg was very popular. But at eighty-four years of age, he was no longer a real force in politics. Hitler saw that one of his main rivals was the current chancellor, Heinrich Brüning. The other was General Kurt von Schleicher, a clever assistant to Hindenburg. Schleicher wanted to replace Brüning as chancellor. Both politicians tried to persuade Hitler to join with them.

Hindenburg ran for reelection as president in 1932. Hitler ran against him. Hindenburg won with more than 19 million votes. Although Hitler lost, he received more than 13 million votes.

Hitler continued to build his organization. The Nazis handed out leaflets and held rallies at which Hitler gave speeches. The Nazis also broadcast Hitler's speeches by radio. Hitler was the first German politician to use aircraft to travel quickly from town to town during election campaigns. His opponents' methods, on the other hand, were slow and outdated.

Brüning disliked and distrusted Hitler and the Nazis. He feared the Nazis would take power by force. The Nazis had 400,000 SA troops, plus another, smaller body of troops called the SS, short for *Shutzstaffel* or defense unit. The Nazis had four times as many troops as the regular German army. Brüning decided to ban the SA and the SS. However, Schleicher convinced Hindenburg to dismiss Brüning as chancellor in May 1932. The ineffective Franz von Papen became chancellor. Hitler was delighted at these events. He offered to support von Papen if the ban on his troops were lifted. Papen agreed.

The Nazis had four times as many troops as the regular German Army.

When the ban was lifted, the Nazis engaged in street warfare with the armed troops of the Communist Party. With this bloody fighting in the background, the Nazis won 37 percent of the vote in the July election. They became Germany's largest party.

Hitler Becomes Chancellor

Hitler demanded that Hindenburg make him chancellor. When Hindenburg refused, Hitler threatened to bring chaos to the streets. In September Papen dissolved the Reichstag and called for new elections. Over several months, the parties competed for power in the Reichstag. The Social Democrats and the Communists combined were stronger than the Nazis. But they failed to unite against their common enemy.

Finally, Schleicher, Papen, and Oskar (Hindenberg's son) persuaded Hindenburg to appoint Hitler as chancellor. Their meeting was secret, so historians are not certain of their motives. The men probably thought they could use Hitler's popularity to their advantage. It is likely they thought they could limit Hitler's actual power. Finally, on January 30, 1933, after years of attempts, Hitler became chancellor.

1933: The End of German Democracy

Franklin D. Roosevelt became president of the United States in January 1933. Most of the world expected Roosevelt to bring many changes. Most political observers, however, did not expect Hitler to bring many changes to Germany. They were wrong.

Hitler was determined to secure all power to himself. After the Reichstag fire, parliament gave emergency powers to Hitler. Now he could pass laws without a vote of parliament. Still, Hitler called another election. He hoped that the Nazis could gain an outright majority of the vote. But the election in March 1933 disappointed him. The Nazis won 44 percent of the vote. They were the largest party, but did not gain a true majority.

Now Hitler began to move boldly against the other parties in parliament. He outlawed the Communist Party. He intimidated the Center Party into supporting him. He had some officials of the Social Democratic Party arrested. This gave the Nazis enough votes to pass a law called the Enabling Act. This law gave full dictatorial power to Hitler. Now there were no limits on Hitler, and he began to ruthlessly destroy his political enemies. Parties that had opposed Hitler, the People's Party and the Social Democratic Party,

He outlawed the Communist Party. He intimidated the Center Party into supporting him. He had some officials of the Social Democratic Party arrested.

were shut down and outlawed. Their leaders were arrested. Then Hitler outlawed the Nationalist Party, the Center Party, and the Bavarian People's Party. In July, all parties except the Nazi Party were banned. It became a crime to engage in politics outside the Nazi Party.

Nazi State Terror

Hitler had cleared away any political competition. Now he began to dominate the rest of German society. He did this through a combination of propaganda, fear, and brute force. He was quite willing to have his opponents murdered. One of Hitler's trusted aides, Herman Göring, was in charge of the police. First he eliminated all Jews and socialists from the police force. Then he made 40,000 SA and SS men into "auxiliary police." They were not interested in protecting law and order. Their job was to crush any remaining opponents of the Nazis.

In 1933 the Germans set up the first concentration camps. Tens of thousands of political opponents were taken there. These early camps, though unpleasant, were actually for detention. It was only later that concentration camps were used for mass murder during the Holocaust.

Also in 1933, the Nazis created a nationwide secret police, the Gestapo. The Gestapo kept information on anyone suspected of opposing the Nazis. They could arrest people for as long as they wanted. They often used torture on prisoners. The courts had no power to intervene. Germany's lawyers, frightened into silence, did nothing.

POLITICAL WORLD — THE ENABLING ACT

After he became chancellor, Hitler wanted to tighten his control over Germany. Some leaders of the SA advised Hitler to seize power by force. It would have been possible, even easy. But Hitler preferred to achieve power by legal methods.

Hitler already had wide-ranging powers granted him after the Reichstag fire. He eliminated the Communists from the Reichstag and reduced the number of Social Democratic Party deputies by arresting them. Hitler needed a two-thirds majority in the Reichstag to pass the Enabling Act. This act would suspend the constitution and give Hitler absolute power.

On March 23 the Reichstag met in the Kroll Opera House. Massed ranks of SA troops surrounded the building. They were there to frighten the deputies. Only eighty-four Social Democrats voted against the bill. The bill passed with 441 votes. Hitler had legally been voted dictator. Democracy in Germany was dead.

THE REICHSTAG FIRE

At 9:00 a.m. on February 27, 1933, a witness saw a man trying to break into the Reichstag, the parliament building in Berlin. A fire broke out soon afterward. By 11:00 a.m. the fire was under control and the police had caught the suspected arsonist. He was a Dutch Communist named Marinus van der Lubbe.

Hitler used the Reichstag fire as the excuse to crush his hated enemies, the Communists. Before dawn on February 28, the SA and police had arrested 4,000 members of the German Communist Party. Lubbe was executed.

The fire had been so convenient that many people suspected that Lubbe was acting on orders from the Nazis. However, historians now believe he was simply a confused terrorist acting alone.

The camps, the Gestapo, the SA, the SS, and the obedient courts gave Hitler all the tools he needed. He could control all aspects of German society. Nazis held all positions of power. Trade unions were abolished. Some businesspeople were allowed to operate without Nazi control. In return they gave money and political support to the Nazis.

Next, Hitler turned to the churches. About one-third of Germans were Roman Catholic and two-thirds were Protestant. Through an agreement with the Pope, the Catholic Church did not criticize the Nazi regime outright (although numerous priests and church members in Germany defied this agreement).

The Protestant churches were harder to control. They were divided and under no central authority. But they spoke out in large numbers against Hitler. In 1935 and 1936, hundreds of Protestant pastors were arrested and imprisoned.

Germany's young people were taught to be loyal to the Nazi government. Most boys joined the Hitler Jugend (Hitler Youth). Most girls joined the BDM (Bund Deutscher Mädel). All other youth groups were banned.

The Nazis also took control of the arts. Opposing books were burned. Books, music, film, radio, and newspapers became tools of the Nazis.

The Nazis also took control of the arts. Opposing books were burned. Books, music, film, radio, and newspapers became tools of the Nazis. Many German artists, writers, and musicians fled to western Europe or the United States, as the cultural life became dull or conformist.

By 1934 every major institution in Germany was subject to *Gleichschaltung*, or coordination. All parts of life had to serve the Nazis and their ideas.

The largest opposition to Hitler now came from within his own party. The leaders of the SA felt that Hitler had pushed them aside. Ernst Röhm, their commander, openly criticized Hitler. On the night of June 29–30, 1934 Hitler struck back. He had the SS and Göring's police arrest Röhm and all other leaders of the SA. They were taken to a prison in Munich and shot. Hitler also had some former political allies murdered. Among them were

General von Schleicher and his wife. This event came to be called the Night of the Long Knives.

This round of executions silenced any remaining opposition to the Nazis. The government now concentrated on building the autobahn (freeway) network and rearmament. These programs reduced unemployment and the economy boomed.

In 1935 the government passed the Nuremberg Laws. These were aimed at Germany's Jews. The laws labeled Jews inferior citizens. Jews could no longer marry non-Jews.

In 1936 there was a period of quiet. The Olympics were held in Berlin. Hitler wanted to create a good impression of the new Germany. There were no new crackdowns on freedom. Of course, by that time there was almost no opposition to the Nazis left within Germany.

The largest opposition to Hitler now came from within his own party. The leaders of the SA felt that Hitler had pushed them aside.

Building a Greater Germany

Hitler had always planned to expand Germany. At a meeting in 1933, he told a group of generals that he planned to seize the Sudetenland, a part of Czechoslovakia. He also planned to annex Austria, defeat France, and conquer Poland and Russia. At the time, these plans were absurd. Germany's military power was pitifully weak.

But Hitler was quite serious. In 1933 Germany withdrew from peace talks in Switzerland and also from the League of Nations. These actions suggested that Germany was not interested in world peace.

Hitler tried to win the Italian dictator, Benito Mussolini, over to Germany's side in 1934. This effort failed. Mussolini was unimpressed with the "Austrian corporal."

The Nazis turned their attention to Austria. Engelbert Dollfuss, Austria's chancellor, disliked the Nazis. He was opposed to the idea of the *Anschluss* (the union of Austria with Germany). Hitler supported an attempt by Austrian Nazis to overthrow the government. Dollfuss was

PERSECUTING GERMANY'S JEWS

There were 650,000 Jews in Germany in 1933. They were fully a part of German society. There was no rational reason to attack them. In the following six years, 490,000 German Jews fled the country.

The Nazis started to target the Jews in 1930. Eight Jews were killed in January of that year. In 1931 the Nazis attacked fifty synagogues and one hundred Jewish cemeteries. After that, Jews were constantly harassed and bullied. In 1935 the racist Nuremburg Laws made life almost impossible.

On the night of November 9, 1938, Hitler unleashed the Nazis Party's armed thugs on Germany's Jewish community. Troops of the SA and SS murdered ninety-one Jews and put 30,000 more into concentration camps. There was great destruction of property as well. Thousands of shops and homes were destroyed. The Nazis burned 190 synagogues. The destruction was known as *Kristallnacht* (Night of the Broken Glass) because of the broken glass left lying in the street.

Passersby look at a storefront with broken glass as a result of *Kristallnacht*.

murdered, but the overthrow failed. Italian leader Mussolini moved his army to the Austrian border. He declared that he would support the Austrian government, and the rest of the world was outraged by the Nazis' aggression. Hitler would have to wait another four years for the union of Austria and Germany.

In 1935 the Saarland, a rich province that had been under French control since World War I, rejoined Germany. Three months later, Hitler announced that Germany would ignore the military restrictions of the Treaty of Versailles. Germany began building an air force, beginning the draft for service in the armed forces and increasing the size of Germany's army and navy.

Hitler tried to improve relations with Britain as a key to his success and as a foundation for his desire to rearm. Some British politicians were openly hostile to the Nazis. However, the British were not interested in a confrontation.

In 1933 Germany withdrew from peace talks in Switzerland and also from the League of Nations.

In 1935 Britain agreed to a new naval treaty. It allowed Germany to build a navy one-third the size of the British. Hitler was pleased at this success. That same year, Mussolini invaded the African country of Ethiopia. Britain and France were outraged at Italy's attack. For the first time, Italy began to look to Germany as a possible ally against Britain and France.

Hitler was ready to take a big gamble and defy the Allies openly. The Rhineland was a strip of German land east of the Rhine River. It lay on the border of France, Belgium, and the Netherlands. The Versailles peace conference made this a demilitarized zone. Germany was not allowed to have any troops there to prevent it from making any surprising attacks on France, Belgium, or the Netherlands.

In 1936 Hitler sent troops into the Rhineland. France and Britain did nothing. This was a major victory for Hitler. Without firing a shot, he had made Germany much stronger. Hitler grew even bolder. Later in 1936, the Spanish Civil War broke out. Hitler and Mussolini supported the Spanish nationalist leader, General Franco. Spain became a battleground to test out new German weapons. In late 1936 Germany signed the Anti-Comintern

N

North Sea

SWEDEN

ESTONIA

DENMARK

Baltic Sea

LATVIA

LITHUANIA

BRITAIN

EAST PRUSSIA

NETHERLANDS

•London

POLAND

Warsaw•

Berlin•

GERMANY

BELGIUM

Rhine River

Dresden•

Sudetenland occupied 1938

Paris

LUX

Prague•

•

CZECHOSLOVAKIA

FRANCE

Danube River

Vienna

SWITZ

Munich•

AUSTRIA

Budapest

Rhineland occupied 1936

HUNGARY

ROMANIA

ITALY

Belgrade•

Austria annexed 1938

YUGOSLAVIA

Mediterranean

Sea

Sofia

Corsica

•Rome

BULGARIA

0   400 miles

ALBANIA

0   700 km

GREECE

Hitler took a gamble when he sent German troops into the Rhineland. If France and Britain had opposed the move, Germany would have backed down. But France and Britain did nothing.

Pact. Germany, Japan, and Italy promised to oppose the Soviet Union. Hitler was almost ready for full-scale war.

German Rearmament

When Hitler became chancellor, the German army was limited to only 100,000 troops. It had no aircraft, heavy artillery, or tanks. Hitler ordered Germany to rearm. First he began to build a new German air force, the *Luftwaffe*, headed by Göring. The country had no pilots or aircraft in 1933. By 1935 it had hundreds of aircraft along with pilots and crews. All of this was forbidden by the Treaty of Versailles. German pilots and planes, known as the Condor Legion, fought in the Spanish Civil War and gained valuable experience. The German Navy also expanded, with several new warships built in the 1930s.

The army increased from 100,000 troops in 1933 to 300,000 in 1935. But it was still a small army when it occupied the Rhineland in 1936. After seeing a demonstration of a tank, Hitler decided that tanks would win future battles. He ordered the army to build large numbers of them. A few German generals decided that the best way to use tanks—known as panzers in German—was massed in large groups. This was a controversial idea, and most German generals did not agree. But Hitler saw the value in massed tanks, and ordered the army to organize panzer divisions. These were large units of tanks that would move quickly and cooperate with attacking aircraft. Germany was becoming ready for war.

▶The Japanese army marches into northern China in 1937. After defeating the Russians in the Russo-Japanese War of 1904 to 1905, the Japanese became increasingly militaristic.

5 Asia Between the Wars

KEY PEOPLE	KEY PLACES
Mohandas Gandhi	Nanking, China
Jiang Jieshi (Chiang Kai-shek)	Peking (Beijing), China
Franklin Roosevelt	Amritsar, India
Sukarno	
Mao Zedong	

The interwar years saw a rise in independence movements among colonies in Asia. At the end of World War I, European countries still ruled large parts of Asia as colonies. In addition, the United States had colonial control over the Philippines. Asia was very poor. Most of its people were farmers.

The peak of Western imperialism was passing. The idea of nationalism was growing throughout Asia. At the same time, Japan was becoming a modern industrial nation with a strong military. The Japanese defeated Russia in a war in 1905. It was the first time in modern history that an Asian country had defeated a European power. As a result of that victory, Japan began to build an empire of its own.

The British Raj

British rule in India dated back to the eighteenth century. There had been challenges to their rule, however. In 1857, sepoys, Indian soldiers in British service, rebelled. Later, the Indian National Congress grew into the main voice of Indian nationalism. It was not until World War I that Indian nationalism mushroomed into a mass movement.

> *It was not until World War I that Indian nationalism mushroomed into a mass movement.*

Because of World War I, many of the old, powerful empires disappeared or lost power. A new world power, the United States, emerged. Its leader, Woodrow Wilson, believed that all people should rule themselves. By the end of the war, the Indian National Congress had made an alliance with the Muslim League, the other major political party in India. In 1918 most Indians called for self-government.

KEY FIGURES

MOHANDAS GANDHI

Mohandas Gandhi (1869–1948) was the father of Indian independence. Born into a a wealthy family, he was educated in England. He became a lawyer in London, where he experienced racism.

After a few years he went to South Africa. Gandhi became a leader in the South African Indian community's fight for civil rights. When he returned to India in 1915, Gandhi led the independence movement there.

In 1920 his followers gave him the title Mahatma, meaning *great-souled*. Gandhi was famous for his stirring speeches and his honesty. He wore simple peasant clothes and reached out to the poorest groups in India. Gandhi based his campaigns on nonviolence.

After World War II, Gandhi helped negotiate independence for India. A year later a Hindu extremist assassinated Gandhi because he had shown goodwill toward Muslims.

With nonviolent tactics, Mohandas Gandhi led India's independence movement for nearly thirty years.

WEBB MILLER

Two weeks after Gandhi was arrested for his anti-salt tax "march to the sea," some of his followers made a similar march. An American news reporter, Webb Miller, watched the British imperial government's response to peaceful civil disobedience:

The salt deposits were surrounded by ditches filled with water and guarded by 400 native Surat police in khaki shorts and brown turbans. Half a dozen British officials commanded them. The police carried lathis—five-foot clubs tipped with steel. Inside the stockade twenty-five native riflemen were drawn up.

In complete silence the Gandhi men drew up and halted a hundred yards from the stockade. A picked column advanced from the crowd, waded the ditches, and approached the barbed-wire stockade... Police officials ordered the marchers to disperse... The column silently ignored the warning and slowly walked forward... Suddenly, at a word of command, scores of native police rushed upon the advancing marchers and rained blows on their heads with their steel-shod lathis. Not one of the marchers even raised an arm to fend off the blows. They went down like tenpins. From where I stood I heard the sickening whacks of the clubs on unprotected skulls... In two or three minutes the ground was quilted with bodies. Great patches of blood widened on their white clothes...

I can understand any government's taking people into custody and punishing them for breaches of the law, but I cannot understand how any government that calls itself civilized could deal as savagely and brutally with nonviolent, unresisting men as the British have this morning.

Soon, two events stirred up public anger in India. The first was a new rule by the British imperial government. It allowed judges to try political cases without juries. It also let provincial governments put political protesters in jail without a trial.

Two events stirred up public anger in India. The first was a new rule by the British imperial government.

The second event was the Amritsar massacre. On April 13, 1919, British troops shot demonstrators protesting the new laws. Nearly 400 Indians died. More than a thousand were wounded. The incident enraged Indians. Before the massacre, Indian leaders such as Mohandas Gandhi called for cooperation with the British. Now he decided that there could be no compromise. His method was non-cooperation, or passive disobedience.

The most dramatic event in Gandhi's campaign was his attack on the salt tax.

The most dramatic event in Gandhi's campaign was his attack on the salt tax. In 1930 he made his famous "march to the sea." He and his followers marched 300 miles (483 km) to the coast. There, he picked up salt from the beach. This was an illegal act. It defied the imperial monopoly on the production of salt. Symbolic acts like this inspired the Indian people to take part in civil disobedience, which emphasized nonviolence.

The civil disobedience movement grew stronger. The British finally gave ground and created a new system of government. India was divided into eleven provinces. Each province had an appointed governor but an elected legislature. Gandhi's Congress Party won majorities in seven of the eleven provinces. It was clear that India would soon become independent. The start of World War II delayed, but could not prevent, this process.

Indonesia

The Netherlands had ruled Indonesia for almost three hundred years.

Indonesia is a group of 3,000 islands in the Pacific Ocean. Covering 3,200 square miles (5,120 sq km), it is the largest country in Southeast Asia. By 1900, its population was more than 60 million. The Netherlands had ruled Indonesia for almost three hundred years. They called Indonesia the East Indies. The islands were a source of great wealth to the ruling country.

Gradually, the Indonesians grew to despise their foreign rulers. The Dutch responded with a few minor reforms. Between 1900 and 1918 they gave Indonesians a voice in local government. They also allowed a national assembly. But it had limited powers. These steps did not go far enough. By the end of World War I, the independence movement was growing.

Under the leadership of Sukarno, the nationalist movement became more radical. The Great Depression caused terrible poverty in Indonesia, and many Dutch residents decided to return home to the Netherlands. This provided even more fuel for the nationalist movement.

In May 1940, German troops occupied the Netherlands. The Dutch colonial authorities in the islands—the governor and his staff—tried to rule on their own. But the Japanese occupied the islands in 1942. Dutch imperialism in Asia was over.

The Great Depression caused terrible poverty in Indonesia, and many Dutch residents decided to return home to the Netherlands.

SUKARNO

KEY FIGURES

Known by his only name, Sukarno (1901–1970) led the Indonesian movement against Dutch rule. He was known as a fiery speechmaker. He always insisted on full independence. During the 1930s he spent periods of time in prison, but he always returned to his cause.

The Japanese took over Indonesia during World War II. Sukarno cooperated with the Japanese puppet government. After the war he became the leading figure in Indonesian politics. He became the first president of the new Republic of Indonesia in 1949. In 1967, army officers overthrew him. He spent the rest of his life under arrest until his death in 1970.

Sukarno

Life in the Philippines

From 1898 to 1946, the Philippines were a U.S. colony. The United States captured the Philippines in the war against Spain in 1898. The island nation gave the United States a valuable military base in the Pacific.

Most Filipinos worked in farming. Sugar cane, rice, and coconuts were the main crops. Poverty and hunger were widespread. Average Filipinos had no real political rights. A handful of wealthy families dominated the country. These plantation owners worked with U.S. businesses. They made huge profits by exporting goods to the United States. They ignored the needs of the common peasants.

In 1916 the United States promised independence for the Philippines at some date in the future. But U.S. authorities did nothing to improve the lives of the Filipino people.

U.S. servicemen and Filipino women in 1919. The United States took control of the Phillipines in 1898 and established several military bases.

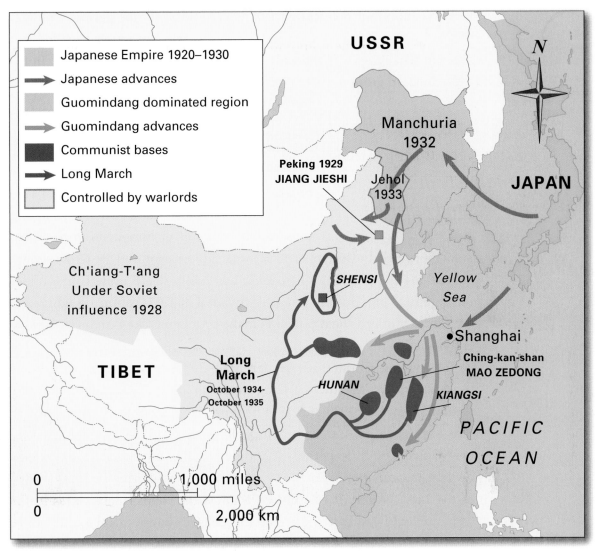

In 1927 negotiations between the Chinese Communists and the nationalists broke down. A civil war broke out soon after.

Civil War in China

For decades, China was torn by civil war and Japanese invasion. The Man-chu empire in China had fallen apart. In 1911 the Republic of China was created. Its first president was Yuan Shikai. But he could not gain control over the whole country. After his death in 1916, local military leaders called warlords fought a civil war across China.

Two important political parties emerged during this period. One was the Nationalist Party or Guomindang, led by Sun Yixian (also spelled Sun Yat-sen). The other was the Communist Party, led by Mao Zedong. In the 1920s the two groups worked together, despite their different ideas. After Sun's death in 1925, Jiang Jieshi (Chiang Kai-shek) became leader of the Guomindang.

Jiang struck first, killing tens of thousands of Communists in Shanghai and other cities.

The Communists and the Guomindang cooperated to fight the warlords. But their alliance broke down in 1926 and 1927. The two groups began to fight each other. Jiang struck first, killing tens of thousands of Communists in Shanghai and other cities. In December 1927 Jiang's forces captured the Chinese capital, Peking (now Beijing). It seemed that Jiang would unite China under the Guomindang. But the Japanese invaded in 1931, capturing northeastern China. Warlords held power in many provinces. The Communists were entrenched in the southwest.

The young Communist leader Mao Zedong worked with China's peasant farmers. Meanwhile Jiang made no attempt to bring democracy to China. Between 1930 and 1934 he worked to crush the Communists in their stronghold in Kiangsi province. To escape, in 1934 Mao led 80,000 of his followers on a desperate 6,200-mile (10,000-km) march. They crossed deserts and mountain ranges to reach a new base. This became known as the Long March. It established Mao as the undisputed leader of the Communists. In addition, it spread the ideas of Communism to millions of ordinary Chinese. This set the stage for a final battle between Communists and nationalists. However, first China had to fight the menace of Japan.

Japanese Ambition

After defeating Russia in 1905, Japan began to expand. In 1910 Japan took over Korea. In 1915 Japan presented China with what were called the Twenty-one Demands. These would have made China a virtual colony of Japan. China chose to resist, and war followed.

By 1918 Japan was industrializing rapidly. International trade was making the country rich. Then the Great Depression damaged world trade. Some Japanese leaders looked to China and the rest of Asia. They saw a source of raw materials for Japanese industry and land for Japan's population to settle. This was similar to Adolf Hitler's idea that Germany needed "living space" in eastern Europe.

JIANG JIESHI (CHIANG KAI-SHEK)

KEY FIGURES

Jiang Jieshi (1887–1975) was the leader of the Chinese Nationalist Party, or Guomindang. As a young man Jiang received military training in Moscow. In 1924 he returned to China and formed the Nationalist Army. He fought against the power of the Chinese warlords.

At first Jiang was backed by the Soviet Union. The Chinese Communists under Mao Zedong cooperated with the Guomindang. But this alliance was always fragile. Jiang had no interest in sharing power with the Communists or giving rights to the workers.

In 1927 Jiang showed his true colors. His troops massacred thousands of Communists. He set up a dictatorship with Nanking as the capital. By crushing the Communists in the cities of China, Jiang forced Mao Zedong to draw support from China's peasants.

Jiang led the nationalists in a long civil war against the Communists. This war ended in Communist victory in 1949. He fled to the island of Formosa (now Taiwan). He led a nationalist government there until his death in 1975.

Jiang Jieshi (Chiang Kai-Shek)

In the 1930s the Japanese government grew more hostile. Japan dropped out of the League of Nations in 1933. In 1934 Japan broke its treaty agreements that limited the size of its navy. In 1936 Japan joined the Anti-Comintern Pact with Nazi Germany. Four years later, Japan joined Germany and Italy in a full-scale military alliance.

By the end of the 1930s, Japan announced it would unite Asia. This would place all Asians under Japanese "leadership." This plan included capturing the Asian colonies of France, Britain, and the Netherlands.

The Sino-Japanese War

China was the first country to suffer from Japanese aggression. Japan conquered Manchuria in 1931. Japan then slowly spread into northern China. By 1935 Japan controlled five northern provinces. In 1937 the Japanese government, which was by then under the control of the army, launched a full-scale operation to conquer all of China.

The invasion began with what has been called the Marco Polo Bridge Incident. At the Marco Polo Bridge on the outskirts of Peking, Japanese troops fired at Chinese soldiers. The Chinese soldiers fired back. This brief skirmish is often considered the opening of World War II in Asia.

With China in danger, Mao Zedong and Jiang Jieshi agreed to stop fighting each other and resist the Japanese. But the Japanese assault was overpowering.

With China in danger, Mao Zedong and Jiang Jieshi agreed to stop fighting each other and to resist the Japanese. But the Japanese assault was overpowering. Shanghai fell to Japanese forces after a heroic three-month resistance. The Japanese forces advanced to Nanking, forcing Jiang and his troops to flee his capital. After the Japanese took the city, they mercilessly killed between 200,000 and 300,000 civilians.

The Japanese generals expected that the Chinese would surrender after the loss of their capital. Instead the war continued. The destruction and loss of life were terrible. As many as 20 million Chinese civilians were left homeless.

By 1938 Japan had conquered China's coast, its major cities, and most of its railroads. Jiang set up a new capital in the western mountains of China. For the rest of the war the nationalists barely did anything to regain the areas under Japanese control. Jiang's policy was to wait for Japan to be defeated by the Western powers.

Meanwhile the Communists fought a guerrilla war against the Japanese. They also helped the Chinese peasants by opening schools and providing medical care. They won the support of many ordinary Chinese people.

POLITICAL WORLD | THE RUSSO-JAPANESE NEUTRALITY TREATY

In August 1939 Hitler announced a nonaggression pact with the Soviet Union. Japan and the Soviet Union were longtime enemies. The pact meant that Stalin could shift troops from his western border. He could strengthen his armies in the east, where the Soviets had battled Japan since 1937. As a result, Japan's leaders gave up on expanding into Soviet territory. Instead they turned away from the Soviet Unit and expanded into Southeast Asia and the Pacific.

The Japanese signed a neutrality pact with the Soviet Union in April 1941. Two months later, Hitler did an about-face and invaded the Soviet Union. The Japanese were pleased. The European powers were entirely busy fighting each other. The Japanese went on with their plan to build an empire in Indochina and the Pacific.

The Soviet Union's large numbers of troops and equipment, such as this T-34 tank, helped convince Japan to sign a neutrality pact.

By 1940 the war was a stalemate. China was divided into three parts. Japan held the north and the coastline. The Communists held the northwest. The nationalists held the south and southwest. For Japan, the focus of the war shifted to Southeast Asia. The outcome there depended on the Western democracies, especially the United States.

The United States in the Pacific

Isolationism was strong in the United States in the 1930s. President Roosevelt repeatedly stated that the United States would stay out of any war in Europe. In response to the Sino-Japanese War, Roosevelt also stayed neutral.

President Roosevelt repeatedly stated that the United States would stay out of any war in Europe.

Roosevelt, along with most Americans, disliked Japanese aggression and sympathized with China. Roosevelt had to avoid any incident that might draw the United States into the Sino-Japanese war. But it was clear that Japan posed a threat.

U.S.–Japanese Friction

On December 12, 1937, Japanese aircraft "accidentally" sank the *Panay*, a small U.S. gunboat on the Yangtze River. This might have led to war if the United States had been in a less isolationist mood. Instead, the U.S. public was satisfied when the Japanese government apologized and paid money to the victims.

Throughout 1937, Japan "accidentally" bombed U.S. churches, hospitals, and schools in China.

Throughout 1937, Japan "accidentally" bombed U.S. churches, hospitals, and schools in China. The goal was to get all Americans to leave China. This effort was largely successful.

Acting together, the British and U.S. governments may have been able to force the Japanese to retreat from the Yangtze valley region of China. But the two countries had no appetite for this effort. Still, Roosevelt knew that the United

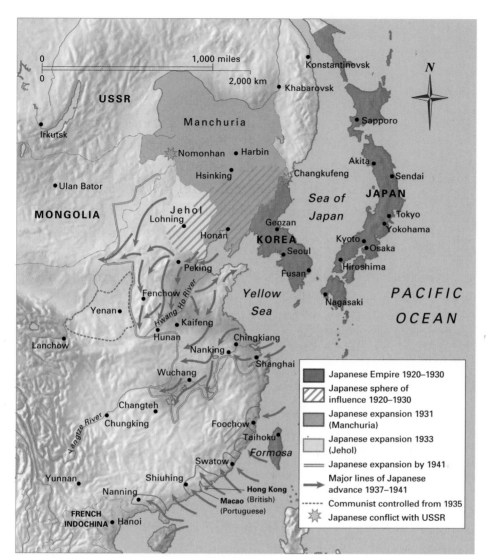

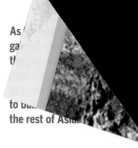

As
ga
th
to b...
the rest of A...

Map Legend:

- Japanese Empire 1920–1930
- Japanese sphere of influence 1920–1930
- Japanese expansion 1931 (Manchuria)
- Japanese expansion 1933 (Jehol)
- Japanese expansion by 1941
- Major lines of Japanese advance 1937–1941
- Communist controlled from 1935
- Japanese conflict with USSR

States had to prepare for possible war with Japan. In 1938 he began to strengthen U.S. defenses in the Pacific. He authorized a loan to the Chinese Nationalist Party.

In 1941 Japan demanded that France give its military bases in Southeast Asia to Japan. This indicated that a wider war was coming. In response, the United States, Britain, and the Netherlands placed a total ban on trade with Japan. This step brought the United States and Japan closer to war.

▶Soldiers in Tanganyika (now Tanzania). Colonial armies were made up of troops of local Africans commanded by white officers.

6 Africa, the Middle East, and Latin America Between the Wars

KEY PEOPLE	KEY PLACES
Arthur Balfour	Iraq
Theodor Herzl	Gran Chaco
Feisal bin al-Hussein	Palestine
Mustafa Kemal	South Africa
	Syria

I n the late 1800s, the major European countries divided Africa among themselves. By 1900 all of Africa was directly or indirectly under European rule except Abyssinia (Ethiopia) and Liberia. At the end of World War I, colonies formerly under German and the Ottoman rule were transferred to the Allies. These colonies became League of Nations mandates.

Britain and France had the largest presence in Africa by far. Britain's African Empire included colonies in East Africa, West Africa, and Southern Africa. The country now known as South Africa became a self-governing dominion in 1910, but remained part of British Africa. The French had a large presence concentrated in northern and western Africa.

Lesser European powers also had colonies in Africa. The Belgian Congo lay in the middle of Africa, while Portugal held Angola and Mozambique to the south. The Italians controlled Libya in North Africa and Eritrea and Somalia on the east coast. Spain had a smattering of small colonies.

Colonialism in Practice

The continent of Africa was organized into some fifty colonies. The colonies' borders were arbitrarily drawn by Europeans without regard to tribal and cultural associations. The colonial powers paid almost no attention to the interests of their African subjects. The common belief at the time was that Europeans were superior to other peoples.

European countries colonized Africa for a number of reasons. As a seafaring empire, Britain wanted strategic ports in Africa. Africa had untapped natural resources and potential new markets for European goods. Many Europeans thought it was their duty to bring Christianity, European medicine, and Western education to the peoples of Africa. The response of Africans to imperialism varied widely. Some fought back, but the Europeans had vast wealth and military strength.

European powers carved up Africa among themselves in the late 1800s. This map shows Africa in 1919, when Germany's colonies were allocated to Britain and France after the Treaty of Versailles.

MOROCCO
TUNISIA
SPANISH MOROCCO
ALGERIA
LIBYA
EGYPT
FRENCH WEST AFRICA
Niger River
NIGERIA
FRENCH EQUATORIAL AFRICA
Nile River
ANGLO-EGYPTIAN SUDAN
ERITREA
ABYSSINIA (Ethiopia)
LIBERIA
TOGOLAND
Jointly administered by Britain and France
CAMEROON
Jointly administered by Britain and France
Congo River
BELGIAN CONGO
BRITISH EAST AFRICA
SOMALILAND
To Britain (formerly German East Africa)
INDIAN OCEAN
ANGOLA
NORTHERN RHODESIA
MOZAMBIQUE
To Britain (formerly German Southwest Africa)
SOUTHERN RHODESIA
Madagascar
BECHUANALAND PROT.
UNION OF SOUTH AFRICA
N

British colonies
French colonies
Italian colonies
Portuguese colonies
Belgian colony
Spanish colonies
Independent
Former German colonies
Borders 1919

0   1,000 miles
0   2,000 km

By the 1920s most colonies had civilian administrations. A typical colony had a governor. He took his orders from the ruling country, although in practice he had almost dictatorial powers. His authority was backed by a colonial army of African soldiers under European officers. Police forces carried out the day-to-day upholding of law and order. These were also made up of Africans commanded by Europeans. There were also civilian officials under the governor. They were responsible for services such as health, education, and public works.

The number of these civil servants was relatively tiny. In Nigeria in the late 1930s, fewer than 1,500 British officials governed some 40 million Nigerians. This meant that the colonial governments relied heavily on African cooperation to function at all.

In Nigeria in the late 1930s, fewer than 1,500 British officials governed some 40 million Nigerians.

In many cases the system worked quite well. Most local chiefs cooperated with colonial wishes. Those who did not were replaced with more cooperative chiefs. Many African traders and farmers saw that they could profit from the new economic arrangements. Many native people found jobs as interpreters, clerks, and servants in the colonial governments. Many more, though, were forced to work in mining and construction projects.

The European treatment of Africans varied during different time periods and in different colonies. Nigeria, for example, had a humane administration. On the other hand, the Belgian Congo was notorious for the cruel treatment of its African workforce.

For those Africans who found jobs in the colonial governments, it was possible to make exceptional progress. Their families received medical care. Their children received at least a basic education and might get a chance to attend a missionary college. On the other hand, to gain these benefits one had to accept the exploitation and racism of the colonial system. A few Africans were even sent to Europe or America to be educated. After World War II this top class of educated Africans would become the leaders of the African nationalist movements.

TECH

An African mine.

Before the colonial period, Africa was exploited through the slave trade. Then the developed world found other ways to exploit the wealth of Africa. In the colonies, cheap African labor was used to develop Africa's natural resources to benefit the colonial powers.

These natural resources were primarily minerals. Africa is very rich in many valuable minerals. By the 1920s Africa was producing more than half the world's gold and almost all the world's diamonds. The continent also holds cobalt, chrome ore, manganese, copper, and tin.

There were also agricultural riches in many African colonies. Colonies grew palm oil, coffee, tea, cocoa, and cotton and shipped these products to the ruling European countries.

South Africa and the ANC

The situation in South Africa was unique. Britain had voluntarily given up political power. The white minorities—the English-speaking community and the Afrikaners, who were of Dutch descent—shared power. Black Africans outnumbered whites four to one. But the country was run entirely for the benefit of whites. Africans were not allowed to own land in 90 percent of the country. This forced black Africans to work on white farms, in mines, and as servants for white families.

Some black Africans—chiefs, church representatives, and educated individuals—began to organize. They formed the African National Congress (ANC) and began to demand equal treatment. In South Africa and elsewhere in Africa, this struggle would take decades.

The Middle East

Even before the end of World War I, the Ottoman Empire was crumbling. The French and the British drew up a modern map of the Middle East, dividing the region between them. When the war ended, the League of Nations approved this division of territories by making them mandates. However, the League specified that the territories should be made ready for independence as soon as was feasible.

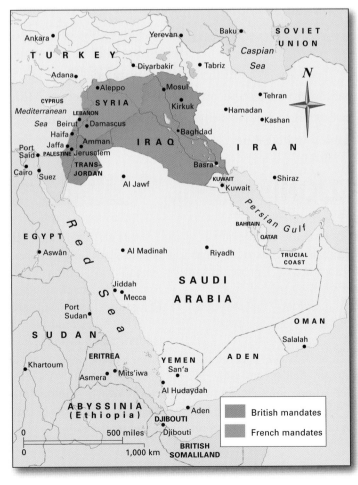

After World War I, with the collapse of the Ottoman Empire, a large region of the Near and Middle East became League of Nations mandates. These mandates were administered by the British and the French.

British Mandate in Palestine

During the war, the Arab tribes had helped the British defeat the Ottoman Turks. The British had promised to support Arab independence after the war. Meanwhile, the British had also promised to support the creation of a "national home" in Palestine for the Jews. This led to conflict in Palestine. Zionists, Jews who demanded a country in Palestine, began moving to Palestine and buying land. They began to create the structure of a Zionist country. Arabs in Palestine feared the Jewish newcomers would take over.

Tens of thousands of Jews moved to Palestine in the 1920s. But when Hitler came to power in Germany, Jewish immigration rose sharply.

In 1920 and 1921, Arabs rioted in Jerusalem, killing several Jews. Jews attacked Arabs in return. A cycle of violence began. In 1929 in a a major incident at the Wailing Wall in Jerusalem, Arab mobs killed 133 Jews, while British police and soldiers killed 110 Arabs.

The Jewish immigration continued. Tens of thousands of Jews moved to Palestine in the 1920s. But when Hitler came to power in Germany, Jewish immigration rose sharply. In 1935 alone, 66,500 Jews moved to Palestine.

POLITICAL WORLD — ZIONISM

Zionism had as its goal the creation of a Jewish state in Palestine. Zionism arose in response to anti-Semitism in Europe in the late 1800s. However, the roots of Jewish nationalism are much older. The idea of a Jewish home in Israel is based in Jewish religious writings.

Theodor Herzl, an Austrian journalist, started the modern Zionist movement. He dreamed of a state where Jews would live in harmony with the Palestinians. Until his death in 1904, Herzl encouraged European Jews to move to Palestine.

In 1917 the British foreign secretary, Arthur Balfour, expressed support for a Jewish homeland in Palestine. He added that the rights of non-Jewish people in Palestine should be protected.

This statement became known as the Balfour Declaration. The statement was open to different interpretations. But it became the basis for Zionist strategy after World War I. The declaration eventually led to the creation of the modern state of Israel in 1948.

Tensions rose. Arabs demanded an end of Jewish immigration and Jewish land purchases. There were more and more acts of violence from both sides. The British had trouble keeping control. From late 1936 to 1939, Palestine was in full-scale revolt. The fighting finally ended in 1939, but tensions remained.

British Mandate in Iraq

In 1920 the region of Mesopotamia, present-day Iraq, was placed under British mandate. Iraq lay between oil-rich Iran and Palestine, with its Mediterranean ports. Also, Iraq had oil fields of its own. Iraq was torn by internal divisions, but all of its religious and tribal groups suddenly united to resist British rule. It took months of fighting before the British could take control. As with their other Middle East mandates, the British looked for an Arab ruler who would follow British orders.

Of all the mandates in the Middle East, Iraq was by far the most successful.

During World War I the British supported Sherif Hussein Ibn Ali. He was one of the most powerful rulers of the Arabian Peninsula. His lands included the sacred Islamic city of Mecca. In 1916 Hussein led the Arab revolt that helped the British defeat the Ottoman Empire.

Hussein expected to become the king of the Arabs. Instead, the British and the French divided up the Arab lands, leaving Hussein with nothing. However, the French chose Hussein's son Abdullah to be king of Transjordan (present-day Jordan). Another son, Feisal, tried to make himself king of Syria. The French quickly expelled Feisal from his new kingdom. The British then chose him to go to Iraq. The Iraqis greeted Feisal as a hero, and he became king of Iraq.

During World War I the British supported Sherif Hussein Ibn Ali.

Feisal was a capable ruler, building up his country. He gradually made Iraq ready for independence, while keeping the support of the British. In 1932 Iraq joined the League of Nations as a fully independent country. Of all the mandates in the Middle East, Iraq was by far the most successful.

French Mandate in Syria

The historical region of Syria included Lebanon, Transjordan, and Palestine. The mandate colony named Syria, created after World War I, was considerably smaller. Syria was under French occupation. As with the British mandates, the French were required to prepare the country for eventual independence.

Syria had several religious and cultural minority groups. Some of these groups welcomed the French presence.

Arab nationalist feeling was strong in Syria. Many Syrians remained angry at the overthrow of Feisal. The French tried to impose a French identity on the country. They made all students learn the French language. The French did little to prepare Syria for self-government.

Syria had several religious and cultural minority groups. Some of these groups welcomed the French presence. They hoped for a modern society based on the French model. The Arab majority, though, strongly demanded Syrian independence.

In 1925 a major revolt broke out. The French responded with unrestrained force. Thousands were killed. The French finally began to prepare Syria for self-government. In 1928 elections were held for a parliament. But the French were not ready to grant independence. Syria was still under French control when World War II began.

POLITICAL WORLD ARAB NATIONALISM

As the Ottoman Empire died, many Arabs began to imagine one country uniting all Arab people. Others supported the creation of several Arab states, based on the ancient kingdoms of the Middle East. Britain and France encouraged these ideas when they were fighting the Ottoman Empire. At the end of the war, they ignored Arab opinion. The steps toward a Jewish homeland in Palestine upset Arabs even more.

The different Arab demands for some form of independence were known as Arab nationalism. This movement became stronger in the years leading up to World War II.

French Mandate in Lebanon

Lebanon was unique in the Middle East. It had a majority Christian population in certain areas. Most of these Christians belonged to the Maronite Church. They supported the French mandate. The Maronites backed the state of Lebanon, whether French-ruled or independent. This would let them be the dominant group. Arab Muslims, on the other hand, wanted to merge Lebanon into a larger Syria or a united Arab state that would take up the whole region.

The Maronites in Lebanon, such as this bishop, had a long association with European Catholicism. They supported the French mandate.

To ease tensions between Maronites and Arab Muslims, the French shared public offices between the two communities. In 1936 the French officially agreed to the goal of Lebanese independence. But World War II broke out, putting independence on hold.

Creation of the Turkish Republic

Turkey became an independent republic. Mustafa Kemal won the presidential election and started the process of modernizing Turkey.

The Ottoman Empire was in ruins at the end of World War I. A peace treaty, the Treaty of Sèvres, was imposed on the Turks in 1920. It stripped away all Ottoman lands outside the heartland of Turkey in Asia Minor. The treaty also divided Turkey itself into British, French, and Italian spheres of influence. Some lands in Asia Minor were given to Greece.

The Turks rose up against this humiliation. Their leader was Mustafa Kemal, later known as Kemal Atatürk. Kemal had been an officer and a war hero in the Ottoman army. He managed to assemble an army and drive the Greeks off Turkish soil. The Italians, French, and British quickly backed down. A new peace conference renegotiated Turkey's borders.

Turkey became an independent republic. Mustafa Kemal won the presidential election and started the process of modernizing Turkey. Kemal stayed in office until the end of his life.

The British in Egypt

When World War I began, the British declared Egypt a British protectorate.

Until World War I, Egypt was officially a province of the Ottoman Empire, but under a strong British influence. British troops were stationed in Egypt. Their most important priority was to protect the Suez Canal. In fact, Egypt was almost a British colony.

When World War I began, the British declared Egypt a British protectorate. After the war, Egyptians wanted to be independent. Violent protests

THE SUEZ CANAL

The Suez Canal links the Mediterranean and the Red Sea. The canal makes it much faster for ships to travel between Asia and Europe. This gives the canal great strategic importance.

The Suez Canal was particularly important to the British government. It was the key link to India and other British possessions in Asia. During World War II the threat of Axis forces seizing the canal was a major factor in British planning.

A merchant ship sails through the Suez Canal, near El Guiser, in 1870. Today the canal is one of the most heavily used shipping lanes in the world.

broke out. In 1922 Britain formally declared Egypt independent. However, the British kept their troops in Egypt, claiming they were necessary to provide security.

Latin America

Latin America prospered after World War I. Europe was recovering from the war. The United States was enjoying strong economic growth. Latin America sold them raw materials and food. The countries of Central and South America went through an economic boom.

The good times came to a halt when Wall Street crashed in late 1929. The world economy collapsed. Latin American exports fell by over one-third in one year—and kept falling. As Latin American economies buckled, their politics became unstable.

During the next decade there were coups—violent overthrows of government—by military officers against elected governments in almost every Latin American country except Mexico. In 1930 the elected governments of

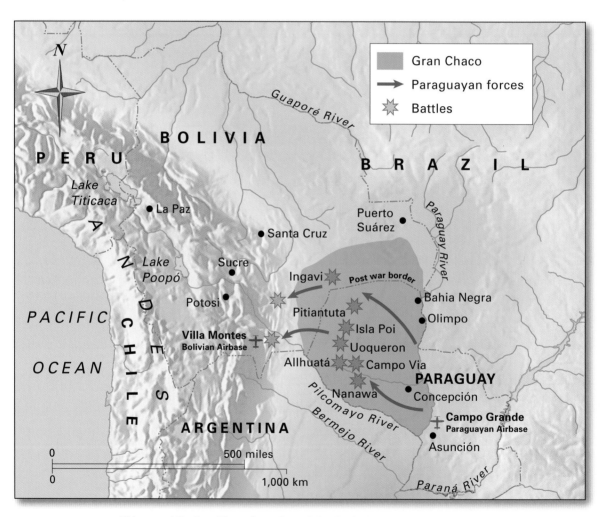

This map of the Gran Chaco shows the main battles in the war between Bolivia and Paraguay from 1932 to 1935. The Gran Chaco was part of Bolivia before the war began. The map shows the present-day borders to illustrate how much territory Paraguay gained in this conflict.

Peru, Argentina, and Brazil were toppled. In the case of Brazil, the military handed over power to a popular politician named Getulia Vargas. He dominated Brazilian politics for the next twenty-five years.

The Chaco War

Relations between countries in Latin America were unstable. At times, minor battles broke out. But in 1932, a major war broke out between Bolivia and Paraguay. At stake was a region called the Gran Chaco. This was a large area on the border between the two countries. It had few inhabitants. When oil was rumored to be found there in 1928, Bolivia's interest was renewed. (Ironically, the oil never materialized.) Access to the Atlantic Ocean via the La Plata river system was another reason Bolivia wanted control of the area.

After four years of fruitless negotiations, Bolivia attacked Paraguay. The Bolivian army was much larger, but the Paraguayans defeated them again and again. In 1935 the Bolivians agreed to a cease-fire. More than 100,000 people died in the fighting. As a result of the war, both countries suffered more military coups.

A Bolivian artillery brigade in November 1932. Despite superior forces, Bolivia was unable to defeat Paraguay.

▶Women and children in England wait in line for bread during the Great Depression.

7 Europe in the 1930s

KEY PEOPLE	KEY PLACES	
Francisco Franco	Abyssinia	London, Great Britain
Adolf Hitler	Sudetenland, Czechoslovakia	Madrid, Spain
Ramsay MacDonald	Rhineland, Germany	
Joseph Stalin		

Under the strain of the Great Depression, democracy struggled. Severe hardship created discontent. Many people became impatient with democratic processes. Totalitarian ideas—Fascism and Communism—gained more followers.

In the 1920s there had been high hopes that there would be no more wars. In the 1930s cooperation between countries unraveled. When the League of Nations was tested, it turned out to be powerless. The high hopes of the 1920s crumbled.

The Great Depression

The Wall Street Crash of 1929 rocked the world economy. Many European countries, including Germany, depended on loans from the United States. When the United States could no longer give out these loans, the damage to its economy spread across the whole world. In every European country, the 1930s were a time of high unemployment.

The Wall Street Crash of 1929 rocked the world economy.

International free trade had grown in the 1920s. It was seen as a way to create prosperity and to bring the nations of the world together for a common goal. But in 1930 the United States sharply increased tariffs, or taxes on imported goods. Other countries quickly did the same. International trade suffered to the disadvantage of almost everyone. When Franklin Roosevelt was elected president, other countries hoped he would ease tariffs to help end the Great Depression, but Roosevelt did not.

Britain

In May 1929, a few months before the Wall Street Crash, Britain held an election. It was the first election in which women under thirty could vote. The result was that the Labour Party won the largest share of the vote, although they did not win a majority of seats in the House of Commons. The Labour Party leader, Ramsey McDonald, became prime minister.

Even before the stock market crash, Britain was faced with a growing problem of unemployment.

Even before the stock market crash, Britain was faced with a growing problem of unemployment. Two million people were out of work. Three years later, the number had risen to nearly 3 million unemployed. To put people to work, the new Labour government began a public works program. This included new roads and houses. When the economic crisis got worse, the government slashed public spending to save money. This action led to a split within the Labour Party. The prime minister formed a coalition government with a part of the Labour Party and other main parties, chiefly the

Conservative Party. This coalition was called the "National Government." It remained in power until 1945.

The British government policy of low taxes and low public spending helped it through the Great Depression. The British used several strategies to do this. One strategy the government used was to devalue, or lower the value of, the British pound. This made British products inexpensive to other countries. So, Britain did not need to add tariffs to goods as the United States and, later, other European countries did. The British stuck to a policy of low taxes, low inflation, and low public spending.

> *Britain did not need to add tariffs to goods as the United States and, later, other European countries did.*

EYEWITNESS

GEORGE ORWELL

George Orwell was a leading English writer in the 1930s. In his book *The Road to Wigan Pier*, he described the life of poor people living in the English town of Wigan.

"I have never seen comparable squalor except in the Far East. But, as a matter of fact, nothing in the East could ever be quite as bad, for in the East you haven't our clammy, penetrating cold, and the sun is a disinfectant.

"Along the banks of Wigan's miry canal are patches of waste ground on which the caravans have been dumped like rubbish hot out of a bucket. . . The majority are old single-decker buses. . . I did not see any that held less than two persons, and some of them contained large families. One, for instance, measuring fourteen feet long, had seven people in it—seven people in about 450 cubic feet of space; which is to say that each person had for his entire dwelling a space a good deal smaller than one compartment of a public lavatory. . .

"Water is got from a hydrant common to the whole colony, some of the caravan-dwellers having to walk 150 or 200 yards for every bucket of water. There are no sanitary arrangements at all. Most of the people construct a little hut to serve as a lavatory on the tiny patch of ground surrounding their caravan, and once a week dig a deep hole in which to bury their refuse.

"All the people I saw in these places, especially the children, were unspeakably dirty, and I do not doubt they were lousy as well. They could not possibly be otherwise."

Authoritarianism and Popular Fronts

One obvious effect of the Great Depression was the rise of authoritarian parties across Europe. Many people began to feel that democracy was ineffective. Authoritarian parties, those calling for dictatorships or Fascism, grew stronger across Europe. Authoritarian groups were already in power in the Soviet Union, Italy, and Poland. In Yugoslavia, King Alexander put down democratic movements. These governments easily survived the shock of the Depression. Other countries came under dictatorships for the first time. Portugal, Bulgaria, and Romania came under right-wing dictatorships. Even Britain and Sweden had Fascist parties, although they never grew large.

Many people began to feel that democracy was ineffective. Authoritarian parties, those calling for dictatorships or Fascism, grew stronger across Europe.

In many countries, there was a similar reaction to the growth of right-wing extremism. In these countries, parties of the center and left joined in alliances called popular fronts. Their common goal was to block the authoritarian parties. Popular fronts took office in Belgium and France in the 1930s.

POLITICAL WORLD — MOSLEY AND BRITISH FASCISM

In the early 1930s an English politician tried to lead a Fascist party into power in that country. Sir Oswald Mosley had been a Conservative member of parliament. Later he switched to the Labour Party. He supported leftist policies of economic planning. His support for what he called "the national spirit" also appealed to some Conservatives.

In 1931 Mosley formed the New Party. When it won no seats in that year's election, Mosley turned to Fascism. In 1932 he renamed his party the British Union of Fascists (BUF). His followers wore black military-style uniforms. At its peak in 1934, the BUF had 20,000 members. They attacked Jews and fought in the street with Communists.

However, the BUF never won a seat in parliament. Sir Oswald and about 760 other former members of the BUF were interned when World War II broke out because of their pro-German sympathies.

Nazism grew in the two places outside Germany with large German-speaking populations: Czechoslovakia and Austria. Three million ethnic Germans lived in the Sudetenland, a part of Czechoslovakia. A Fascist party, supported by the Nazis in Germany, gained strength among the Sudeten Germans. In Austria, the Nazis grew popular as well. Riots and lawlessness spread, weakening the democratic government. In 1934 Nazis assassinated the Austrian chancellor, Engelbert Dollfuss. The country was ripe for a Nazi takeover.

In many countries, parties of the center and left joined in alliances called popular fronts. Their common goal was to block the authoritarian parties.

Corporatism in Italy

The governments of Germany, Italy and the Soviet Union tried to control every part of the lives of their people. The word "totalitarianism" was used to describe them. These governments made use of new technology. They used radio and movies to shape public opinion. They also controlled the education system. Secret police kept watch over the ordinary people. In Italy, political parties other than the Fascists were illegal. Thousands of people were put in prison every year for their political ideas. In 1938 Mussolini began to target Italy's Jews. Jews could no longer marry non-Jews. Jews were also banned from having certain jobs, including teaching and law.

These governments made use of new technology. They used radio and movies to shape public opinion. Secret police kept watch over the ordinary people.

Mussolini's system of running the economy was known as corporatism. New labor organizations were created in 1926. They were called corporations, and the replaced the old trade unions. The corporations included both workers and management. In effect, the workers lost the power to demand better wages or working conditions. Strikes became illegal. Disputes were settled by the government. In effect, workers lost the right to bargain for better wages or conditions of employment.

This propaganda poster for Italian Fascism shows two hands raised in a Fascist salute.
The slogan on the poster reads: "Everything and everyone for victory."

THE CONQUEST OF ABYSSINIA

In October 1935, against the advice of the Italian King Victor Emmanuell III and most of the Italian generals, Mussolini launched an invasion of the African country of Abyssinia, now know as Ethiopia. Mussolini was eager to gain territory in Africa. He also wanted to win glory for his country.

The Italians used aircraft, modern weapons (including poison gas), and a huge army of 600,000 troops. They quickly defeated the Abyssinians, who were led by Emperor Haile Selasse. He fled to England. Abyssinia was combined with two smaller Italian colonies to form the new colony of Italian East Africa.

Italy's aggression troubled the world. Abyssinia was a member of the League of Nations. The League voted to punish Italy with economic sanctions, or bans on imports. Italy depended on imported oil, but oil was not included in the sanctions.

The League never even considered sending military help to Abyssinia. The Italian invasion of Abyssinia effectively marked the death of the League of Nations. The organization had proven that it was too weak to maintain international peace and security.

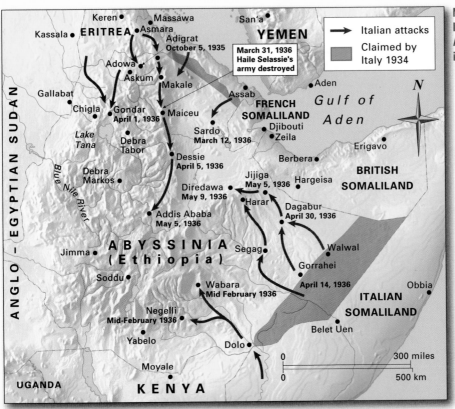

Map of the successful Italian invasion of Abyssinia (Ethiopia) in 1935 to 1936.

Mussolini spread the idea that he was making the Italian economy strong. He did this through propaganda, slanted information to influence an audience. Many people outside Italy believed that the Italian economy was shaking off the Depression. In fact, Mussolini's program of public works was much less successful than Franklin Roosevelt's New Deal. Italian relief for those out of work was limited. In 1934 an unemployed Italian received the equivalent of about five cents a day. In Britain the equivalent was about twenty-five cents. In the United States it was about fifty cents.

In fact, Mussolini's program of public works was much less successful than Franklin Roosevelt's New Deal. Italian relief for unemployed workers was limited.

Partly to distract from the Depression, Mussolini invaded Abyssinia (Ethiopia) in 1935. War created jobs and gave people a focus. The Abyssinian conflict stirred up imperial pride among Italians. It also created tensions with Britain and France—which eventually lead to war.

The Spanish Civil War

Civil war raged in Spain from 1936 to 1939. It began with military uprisings against the Republican government. The rebels could not win complete control of the country. Civil war followed. The two sides reflected how Spanish society was divided. The rebels, or nationalists, were supported by Spain's Fascist party (the Falange), the Catholic Church, wealthy busi-

This vintage stamp depicts General Francisco Franco, who came to power after the Spanish Civil War.

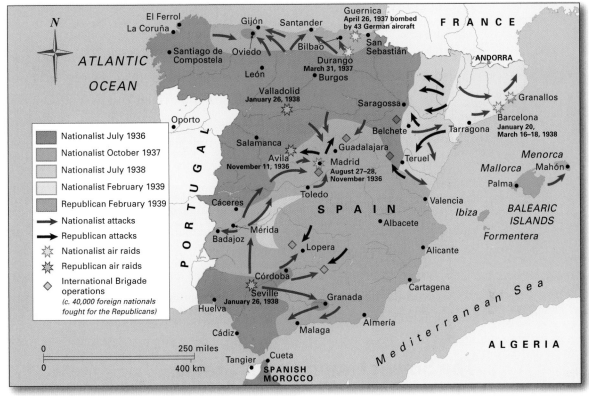

Map showing the progress of the Spanish Civil War (1936–1939).

nessmen, and most of the army's high-ranking officers. The Republican side included moderate liberals, Communists, and anarchists.

Francisco Franco became the leader of the nationalists. He set up a government with himself as head of state. The people of Europe and the world looked on as fighting raged. Many people realized that the two sides mirrored the divisions in many other European countries. It seemed that the war in Spain might be the forerunner of a larger European war.

It seemed that the war in Spain might be the forerunner of a larger European war.

The democratic governments of Britain and France wanted to keep the war from spreading. They were uncomfortable with the presence of Communists among the Republicans. They chose not to intervene in the war. In the United States, isolationist feelings had the same effect. But volunteers from France, Britain, the United States, and other countries traveled to Spain. They formed the International Brigade, fighting for the Republicans.

The war ended in March 1939. The nationalists finally took Madrid, the capital. It probably would have ended sooner, but both sides received outside assistance. The Soviet Union sent military equipment to help the Republicans. However, Germany and Italy assisted the nationalists to a greater degree. Italy sent almost 80,000 Italian soldiers. Germany sent one hundred bomber aircraft. For the Germans, this was a valuable chance to test new equipment. The world was shocked when the Nazis bombed the small town of Guernica, in northern Spain, in 1937.

For the Germans, this was a valuable chance to test new equipment.

The war also helped draw the leaders of Germany and Italy together. They communicated regularly during the Spanish conflict. The two right-wing totalitarian governments soon formed a strong alliance.

The Soviet Union under Stalin

In the 1930s Soviet leader Joseph Stalin conducted a war against his own people. Stalin was determined to make the USSR an industrial heavyweight. The government developed plans to build industry. By 1939 the Soviet Union had grown to the world's third-largest industrial producer, after the United States and Germany.

THE ANTI-COMINTERN PACT

KEY EVENTS

In the mid-1930s Japan was looking for allies. The balance of power in Europe seemed to be shifting away from France and Britain. Japanese army leaders admired Germany, and the army was in control of the Japanese government. In 1936 the two countries agreed to the Anti-Comintern Pact.

Officially, this was an agreement to fight the threat of Communism. But Germany also agreed not to get in the way of Japanese advances in Asia. Italy joined the pact in 1938, and in 1940 the three countries joined the Tripartite Pact. They promised to help each other against an enemy.

Peasants from villages around Moscow view a poster depicting some wealthier peasants as pigs.

The Soviet people received little benefit from their labor. Wages were kept low, and few goods were made for them. Workers who did not meet their production targets were punished and were often sent to labor camps. The chain of forced labor camps eventually became known as the Gulag Archipelago. Many camps were in Siberia, a harsh area of the eastern Soviet Union. In 1929 there were perhaps 500,000 prisoners. By 1945 there were 9 million.

Also important in Stalin's plans was agriculture. Farmers had to grow enough food to feed the factory workers, themselves, and for export. They also had to pay high taxes. In the 1920s most farms were small family farms. Despite the best efforts of the farmers, they could not meet their production targets. So, in 1929 and 1930 Stalin forced all farms under government control. Small farms would be joined to form huge farms called collectives. Stalin thought that a collective would produce more food.

The better-off peasants, called kulaks, suffered greatly during this time. Stalin considered them "enemies of the revolution." Troops seized their farms. It is thought that more than 5 million kulaks were shot, relocated to forced labor camps, or deported to less populated areas of the Soviet Union, including Siberia. In retaliation, many kulaks burned their crops and destroyed their livestock.

During collectivization, as this time is now known, it is estimated that 14.5 million peasants died. But the real number will never be known.

Combined with poor harvests, this resulted in a devastating famine from 1932 to 1934. Millions of peasants died of starvation, including 5 million in the Ukraine alone. During collectivization, as this time is now known, it is estimated that 14.5 million peasants died. But the real number will never be known. "No one was keeping count," said Nikita Krushchev, the future Soviet leader.

At the same time, Stalin decided to clear out any rival, or potential rival, within the Communist Party. These were called Stalin's purges. Many high-ranking Soviet leaders and military officers were killed. Hundreds of thousands of Stalin's enemies were sent to the Gulag. The actual number of people killed was in the millions.

Dealing with Germany

As his power increased, Hitler grew more aggressive. In 1933 he withdrew from the Geneva Disarmament Conference. Soon after that he took Germany out of the League of Nations.

In 1936 Germany sent troops in to the Rhineland. This was forbidden by the Versailles Treaty. It was a calculated gamble by the German leader. If France or Britain made a move to stop the reoccupation, Hitler would have backed down. Germany's military was still too weak to resist.

Military strength		Germany	Britain	France	USSR
Army	1932	100,000	192,000	350,000	562,000
	1939	730,000	237,000	500,000	1,900,000
Military Aircraft	1932	36	445	400	2,595
	1939	8,295	7,940	3,163	10,382
Major Warships	1932	26	284	175	89
	1939	88	290	161	101

Rearm…
the ma…
in Eur…
1932 …

But neither France nor Britain acted. Hitler learned that the two strongest European democracies would do almost anything to avoid a war. The reoccupation meant that Hitler could build defenses along Germany's western border. With this protection in the West, Germany could send troops into eastern Europe.

Hitler learned that the two strongest European democracies would do almost anything to avoid a war.

Many historians believe that 1936 was the last point at which Hitler's aggression could have been stopped and World War II prevented.

The graph above shows the rearmament of the major powers in Europe between 1932 and 1939. The numbers reflect the growing tensions of the period.

▶Austrian soldiers return the Nazi salute of the crowd in March 1938 after the *Anschluss* or annexation of Austria by Germany. It was an ominous sign of things to come.

8 Europe in Crisis, 1938 to 1939

KEY PEOPLE	KEY PLACES	
Neville Chamberlain	Sudetenland, Czechoslovakia	Gleiwitz (Gliwice), Poland
Édouard Deladier	Munich, Germany	Polish Corridor, Poland
Adolf Hitler	Danzig (Gdansk), Poland	
Joachim von Ribbentrop		

In 1936 Germany brashly reoccupied the Rhineland, which had been part of the German Empire prior to World War I. The Allies did nothing in response.

Emboldened, Hitler began other European conquests. He started by annexing Austria in March 1938 and continued with the invasion of Poland on September 1, 1939. Finally, Britain and France declared war on Germany.

The Annexation of Austria

After the successful reoccupation of the Rhineland, Hitler looked to Austria. Austria had been part of the Austro-Hungarian Empire, and the people who lived there spoke German. Culturally, the Austians and Germans were similar. After World War I the people of Austria had wanted to unite with Germany. This joining together is usually referred to as the Anschluss—the German word for union. But the Treaty of Versailles did not allow it.

On March 13, 1938, Hitler announced that Austria was now another province of the German Reich.

A native-born Austrian, Hitler looked forward to adding Austria to the expanding German Reich. Such a union with Germany would add Austria's population and industrial resources to Germany's military machine.

In 1934 the Nazis unsuccessfully tried to take over Austria. This was in part because Italy rushed troops to its border with Austria. At that time, Italy wanted to keep Austria as a buffer between themselves and the growing German Reich.

The Nazi Party continued to exist in Austria, however, funded by Germany. In 1938 Hitler and a more powerful Germany tried again. This time Italy did not interfere.

On February 12, 1938, Hitler invited the Austrian chancellor to his mountaintop headquarters in southern Germany. Once there, Hitler spent eleven hours insulting and threatening the Austrian leader. Hitler demanded that the Austrian Nazis be given positions in government. If not, Germany would invade.

Within days, Austria gave in to Hitler's demand. But then Hitler demanded that the Austrian Nazi leader Arthur Seyss-Inquart be named chancellor of Austria. As soon as the Nazi was in office, he "invited" German troops into the country. On March 13, 1938, Hitler announced that Austria was now another province of the German Reich. In April of that year, an Austrian plebiscite, or vote, was held and, unsurprisingly, the Anschluss was approved with 99.7 percent of the votes cast.

FORMING THE AXIS ALLIANCE

The major countries of the Axis alliance were Nazi Germany, Fascist Italy, and the Empire of Japan. Three treaties bound them together: the Anti-Comintern Pact (November 1936), the Pact of Steel (May 1939), and the Tripartite Pact (September 1940).

The Anti-Comintern Pact was a reference to the Communist International, or Comintern. The Comintern was an organization that aimed to spread Communism beyond the Soviet Union. In the Anti-Comintern Pact, Germany and Japan (and later, Italy) agreed to share information about the Comintern. Hitler was eager to bring Japan into an anti-Soviet alliance.

The Pact of Steel was an alliance between Germany and Italy that was signed in 1939. The two countries agreed to help each other if either one were attacked. The Italians mistakenly signed on the verbal understanding that neither power would start a war before 1943. However, Japan refused to join this pact, which made it less effective.

Germany, Italy, and Japan signed the Tripartite Pact in 1940. They hoped that the pact would intimidate the United States. They wanted the U.S. to stay on the sidelines as war spread. Instead, the United States increased its aid to the Chinese forces fighting Japan. In late 1940 and 1941, six smaller countries also signed the Tripartite Pact.

The Axis alliance never worked very well. Italy, Germany, and Japan never cooperated closely. They had different ideas about how the war should be fought. On the other hand, the Allies—especially Britain and the United States—cooperated very closely.

A collection of Axis propaganda, used to influence world opinion about Germany, Italy, and Japan.

The Czech-German Crisis

Hitler argued that the Anschluss was a logical reunification of German-speaking peoples. Some thought that this supported one of Woodrow Wilson's Fourteen Points with respect to self-determination. Still others, especially in Britain and France, were willing to give in to Hitler's demands to prevent another war. This was called the policy of appeasement. But appeasement only encouraged Hitler to keep annexing more territory.

Appeasement only encouraged Hitler to keep annexing more territory.

Hitler's next target was the Sudetenland, part of Czechoslovakia. This strip of land ran along the border with Germany. Most of the people there spoke German, but these Sudeten Germans had never been part of Germany. However, Hitler claimed they were an oppressed minority who were begging for union with Germany.

Nazis among the Sudeten Germans stirred up unrest. In response, the Czech government sent soldiers to the German border. This let the Germans claim that Czechoslovakia was creating a provocation, or threat. In May 1938, Hitler told his generals to prepare for war in October. The crisis in Sudentenland rumbled on through the summer of 1938 as Germany finalized its plans for war.

The Munich Agreement

The world looked to France or Britain to do something to stop Hitler. The prime minister of Britain was Neville Chamberlain. He felt that Czechoslovakia should give up land to Germany. Chamberlain thought that once Hitler had gained the Sudetenland, he would not make any more demands. But Hitler viewed this policy as a sign of weakness.

The world looked to France or Britain to do something to stop Hitler.

The British proposed a compromise plan in August 1938 that included nearly all of the Sudeten German demands. The Sudeten

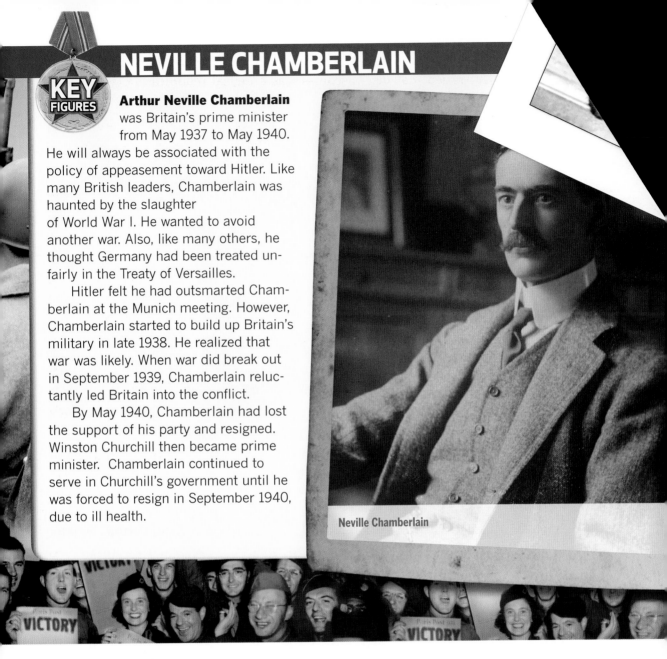

NEVILLE CHAMBERLAIN

KEY FIGURES

Arthur Neville Chamberlain was Britain's prime minister from May 1937 to May 1940. He will always be associated with the policy of appeasement toward Hitler. Like many British leaders, Chamberlain was haunted by the slaughter of World War I. He wanted to avoid another war. Also, like many others, he thought Germany had been treated unfairly in the Treaty of Versailles.

Hitler felt he had outsmarted Chamberlain at the Munich meeting. However, Chamberlain started to build up Britain's military in late 1938. He realized that war was likely. When war did break out in September 1939, Chamberlain reluctantly led Britain into the conflict.

By May 1940, Chamberlain had lost the support of his party and resigned. Winston Churchill then became prime minister. Chamberlain continued to serve in Churchill's government until he was forced to resign in September 1940, due to ill health.

Neville Chamberlain

VICTORY

VICTORY

German leader Konrad Heinlein rejected the plan. Hitler continued to make statements demanding that the Sudetenland become part of Germany. Soon, riots broke out in the Sudetenland. As German troops massed at the border, the Czechs prepared to resist.

The 1938 Munich Peace Conference was attended by Britain's Neville Chamberlain, French leader Édouard Daladier, Germany's Adolf Hitler, and Italian leader Benito Mussolini.

War between Germany and Czechoslovakia seemed likely at any moment. So Chamberlain called for an international conference. British, German, French, and Italian representatives attended. The meeting was held in Munich on September 29–30, 1938. The Czechs were not invited.

The Munich settlement gave Germany everything it wanted. The Czechs were told to evacuate the Sudetenland. Chamberlain flew home and declared "peace in our time" while holding up the Munich Agreement for the news cameras. The eventual result was the destruction of Czechoslovakia. The Munich settlement also encouraged Hitler. He believed that Britain and France would continue to back down if he made more demands.

The German Takeover of Bohemia and Moravia

The Munich Agreement had three results. First, Czechoslovakia began to break apart. The country's other national minorities, the Slovakians and Ruthenians, started demanding self-government. At the same time, Hungary claimed territory in southern Czechoslovakia.

Second, on March 15, 1939, Germany occupied the rest of Czechoslovakia (Bohemia and Moravia), declaring a protectorate. This made it clear that Hitler was not going to stop his expansion. That same month, Hitler forced Lithuania to give up the city of Memel to Germany.

Appeasement was useless when dealing with Hitler. He respected only force.

Third, Hitler grew more confident because Britain and France barely protested these actions. Hitler believed that the western democracies did not have the stomach for war. Appeasement was useless when dealing with Hitler. He respected only force.

POLITICAL WORLD — APPEASEMENT VERSUS REARMAMENT

Appeasement was the policy used by the British to deal with Hitler and Mussolini in the 1930s. Appeasement arose from a wish to avoid another bloody war. The British also needed to cut defense costs. In addition, there was also a widespread feeling in Britain that the Treaty of Versailles had been too harsh on Germany. Many people believed that if Germany and Italy's demands were met, their aggression would stop. There would be peace.

Later, most politicians condemned appeasement as a cowardly policy. It sacrificed smaller countries in a futile attempt to prevent war. Critics also pointed to the failure to rearm. In the case of Britain, this led the country to the brink of defeat in 1940.

The Munich Agreement caused intense debate in Britain. Winston Churchill led the call for rearmament. As Hitler continued his expansion, the British realized that appeasement had been a huge mistake. In late 1938 Britain began building weapons as quickly as possible. In 1939 Britain promised to protect Poland and Romania against future German aggression.

After Munich: Franco-German Pact and Franco-Italian Crisis

After Munich, England tried to improve relations with Italy but was not successful. France realized that Germany now dominated eastern Europe. In December 1938 the German foreign secretary, Joachim von Ribbentrop, went to Paris. The two countries signed a declaration calling for good relations between them. Ribbentrop later claimed that the French had agreed that Germany could now control eastern Europe. The declaration really meant nothing, and tensions continued to rise between the two countries.

> *In 1938 Italy laid claim to the French city of Nice, the French island of Corsica, and French colonies in Africa.*

In 1938 Italy laid claim to the French city of Nice, the French island of Corsica, and French colonies in Africa. But this time France responded strongly, warning Italy to back off. The French leader, Édouard Deladier, went on public visits to the areas claimed by Italy. France's reaction caused Italy to back down. But when Italy attacked Albania, once again the French and British did nothing.

Italy Invades Albania

Germany had expanded into several areas. Italy wanted to expand as well. It looked to the Balkans, and Albania in particular, as an obvious target.

Albania was small, weak, and had few allies. On April 7, 1939, one month after Hitler invaded Czechoslovakia, Mussolini invaded Albania. One hundred thousand Italian troops quickly crushed Albania resistance. The Albanian king fled to Greece.

> *In October 1940, Italian forces in Albania invaded Greece.*

The capture of Albania was a victory for Italy. But it soon led to disaster. In October 1940, Italian forces in Albania invaded Greece. The smaller Greek army soundly defeated the Italians. This forced Germany to invade Yugoslavia and Greece to help the Italians in 1941. This distraction turned out to be costly for Germany's war effort.

Danzig and the Polish Corridor

Germany had maintained good relations with Poland for most of the 1930s. Hitler promised the Poles that Germany had no wish to capture the Polish Corridor and the port of Danzig. These were areas that had been taken from Germany after World War I. Both had large German populations. Almost 1 million Germans lived within the Polish borders after 1919. Considering how Germany had used the presence of German minorities as a reason to annex Austria and Czechoslovakia, the Poles were obviously concerned.

Almost 1 million Germans lived within the Polish borders after 1919.

Poland regarded Germany with caution. Poland joined alliances with France and with the Soviet Union. The Poles hoped these alliances would protect them from their aggressive neighbor.

In March 1939 the Rhineland, Czechoslovakia, and Austria were securely in German hands. Hitler now turned his attention to Poland. Britain and France had promised to protect Poland from German expansion. It seemed that the western democracies were finally willing to stand up to Hitler.

Guaranteeing Poland's Integrity

By March 1939 the Germans were preparing for action against Poland. But this time the British were ready to take steps to block further German aggression. The Poles had no intention of being taken over by Germany. They made it clear they were willing to fight rather than give up territory. The Germans were surprised to encounter a neighbor they could not easily bully.

The Poles had no intention of being taken over by Germany. They made it clear they were willing to fight rather than give up territory.

By now, Britain and France had given up on the policy of appeasement. They promised to defend Poland if Germany attacked. The stage was now set for the start of World War II.

The German-Soviet Pact

On March 30, 1939, Britain guaranteed Poland's independence. Britain and France then offered to sell Poland weapons. To Hitler, this was a direct challenge. Poland stood in the way of German expansion.

In April 1939 Hitler told the German army to prepare to invade Poland. The Allies' guarantee to Poland did not deter Hitler as Chamberlain hoped it would. Britain and France were far away from Poland. Hitler knew that only the Soviet Union could help Poland immediately if a war started.

The USSR had a powerful military. Both Germany and the western democracies approached Joseph Stalin in 1939. Each wanted the USSR on their side. But the British were uncomfortable negotiating with Communist Russia. Their talks broke down.

The expansion of the Greater German Reich in the years 1938 and 1939.

Meanwhile Germany made the Soviets a tempting offer. They would let the Soviets take over eastern Poland, the Baltic States, and parts of Romania. In return, the Soviets would have to agree to Germany's occupation of western and central Poland.

Britain and France were far away from Poland. Hitler knew that only the Soviet Union could help Poland immediately if a war started.

On August 23, 1939, the German foreign secretary, Ribbentrop, and the Soviet foreign secretary, V.M. Molotov, announced the new German-Soviet nonaggression pact. The world was stunned.

Even though sections of the treaty were kept secret, it was clear that the USSR would no longer act as a counterbalance to Germany. The treaty would allow the Germans to continue with their plan to invade Poland. War was now imminent.

The Gleiwitz Incident: Pretext for War

Poland still resisted German demands that it give up land. The Germans needed some excuse for war. The German city of Gleiwitz was located near the Polish border. It became the setting of an extraordinary hoax.

In August 1939, German SS troops forced concentration camp inmates to dress in Polish army uniforms before giving them lethal injections. The bodies were shot and left near the Gleiwitz radio station after a mock raid by SS soldiers, also dressed in Polish uniforms.

Hitler claimed that Poland had attacked Germany. Many observers suspected it was a trick. But Hitler used this as the reason for war. The first German panzer tanks rolled over the Polish border on September 1, 1939.

On September 3, 1939, Britain and France declared war on Germany. The Soviet Union invaded eastern Poland, allowing Germany to capture the western part of Poland. World War II had officially begun.

Timeline

1914-1918 World War I, "the Great War," takes place in Europe, the Middle East, and Africa

1916 Civil war in China

1917 Russian Revolutions ends Russian monarchy; Vladimir Lenin overthrows temporary government; Balfour Declaration announces support of a Jewish homeland

1918 World War I ends on November 11, Armistice Day; U.S. president Woodrow Wilson proposes his Fourteen Points

1919 Treaty of Versailles redraws the map of Europe and calls for creation of the League of Nations; Prohibition becomes U.S. law; Amritsar Massacre takes place in India

1920 Mesopotamia region (Iraq) placed under British mandate

1920-1921 Poland attacks Russia; war ends with Treaty of Riga

1921 Greece invades Turkey but is defeated

1921-1922 Nine nations meet at the Washington Conference

1922 Benito Mussolini and the Fascist Party rise to power in Italy

1926 Germany joins the League of Nations

1928 Sixty-five countries sign the Kellogg-Briand Pact, agreeing to avoid war except for defense

1929 Wall Street crashes; beginning of the Great Depression

1930 Mohandas Gandhi leads the "march to the sea" on India's coast

1932 Franklin D. Roosevelt elected president of the United States; begins the New Deal programs in his first 100 days in office, beginning in January 1933; Iraq joins the League of Nations

1932-1934 Devastating famine in the Soviet Union

1932-1935 Chaco War between Bolivia and Paraguay

1933 Hitler appointed Reich Chancellor by President von Hindenburg; Nazis pass the Enabling Acts; Germany and Japan withdraw from the League of Nations

1934-1935 Mao Zedong leads the Long March

1935 Mussolini declares himself dictator of Italy; the Nazi government passes the Nuremberg Laws; reactivation of the *Luftwaffe* (German air force); 66,500 German Jews emigrate from Germany to Palestine

1935-1936 Italy invades Abyssinia (Ethiopia)

1936 The Olympic Games held in Berlin; Hitler sends troops into the Rhineland; Germany signs the Anti-Comintern Pact with Japan

1936-1939 Spanish Civil War

1937 Sino-Japanese War

1938 *Anschluss* (annexation) of Austria; Munich Agreement; *Kristallnacht* (Night of Broken Glass); Franco-German Pact

1939 Germany and Italy sign the Pact of Steel; German-Soviet Pact; Hitler invades Poland; Britain and France declare war on Germany; World War II officially begins

Bibliography

Arnold, Simone. *Facing the Lion: Memoirs of a Young Girl in Nazi Europe.* New Orleans, Louisiana: Grammaton Press, 2000.

Bell, P. M. H. *The Origins of the Second World War in Europe.* New York: Longman, 1986.

Brenan, Gerald. *The Spanish Labyrinth: An Account of the Social and Political Background of the Spanish Civil War.* New York: Longitude, 1991.

Brendon, Piers. *The Dark Valley: A Panorama of the 1930s.* New York: Alfred A. Knopf, 2000.

Charmley, John. *Chamberlain and the Lost Peace.* New York: Ivan R. Dee, 1989.

Cole, Wayne S. America First: *The Battle against American Intervention 1940–1941.* Madison, Wisconsin: University of Wisconsin Press, 1953.

Corum, James S. *The Roots of Blitzkrieg.* Lawrence, Kansas: University Press of Kansas, 1992.

Davidson, Eugene. *The Making of Adolf Hitler: The Birth and Rise of Nazism.* Columbia, Missouri: University of Missouri Press, 1997.

Deighton, Len, and Walther K. Nehring. *Blitzkrieg: From the Rise of Hitler to the Fall of Denmark.* London: Triad/Granada, 1980.

Dorn, Frank. *The Sino-Japanese War, 1937–1941: From Marco Polo to Pearl Harbor.* London: Macmillan, 1974.

D'Este, Carlo. *Eisenhower.* New York: Owl Books (Henry Holt), 2003.

D'Este, Carlo. *Patton: A Genius for War.* New York: Perennial, 1996.

Evans, Mark L. *Great World War II Battles in the Arctic.* Westport, Connecticut: Greenwood Publishing Group, 1999.

Gilbert, Martin. *Israel: A History. New York:* William Morrow, 2002.

Gilbert, Martin. *The Righteous.* New York: Henry Holt, 2003.

Gilbert, Martin. *Second World War: A Complete History.* New York: Henry Holt, 1989.

Guderian, Heinz. *Achtung—Panzer! The Development of Tank Warfare.* London: Cassell Military Press, 2000.

Heinrichs, Waldo. *Threshold of War: Franklin D. Roosevelt and American Entry into World War II.* New York: Oxford University Press, 1990.

Hitler, Adolf. *Mein Kampf* (translated by Ralph Manheim). Boston: Houghton Mifflin, 1998.

Hogg, Ian. *Great Land Battles of World War II.* London: Blandford Press, 1987.

Johnson, Eric A. *Nazi Terror: The Gestapo, Jews, and Ordinary Germans.* New York: Basic Books, 2000.

Kaplan, Marion A. *Between Dignity and Despair: Jewish Life in Nazi Germany* (Studies in Jewish History). New York: Oxford University Press, 1998.

Keegan, John. *The Second World War.* New York: Penguin Books, 1990.

Kershaw, Ian. *Hitler, 1889–1936: Hubris.* New York: W.W. Norton & Company, 2000.

Kershaw, Ian, and Moshe, Lewin, (eds.). *Stalinism and Nazism: Dictatorships in Comparison.* New York: Cambridge University Press, 1997.

Kimball, Warren F. *Forged in War: Roosevelt, Churchill, and the Second World War.* New York: Ivan R. Dee, Inc., 2003.

Lamb, Richard. *The Drift to War 1922–1939*. New York: St. Martin's Press, 1991.

Laqueur, Walter. *Weimar 1918–1933*. New York: Sterling Publications, 2002.

Lewis, Frederick. *Since Yesterday: The 1930s in America, September 3, 1929–September 3, 1939*. New York: HarperCollins, 1986.

Liddell Hart, Basil. *A History of the Second World War*. New York: DaCapo Press, 1999.

Lindemann, Albert S. *Anti-Semitism before the Holocaust*. New York: Addison-Wesley, 2000.

Lord, Walter. *Day of Infamy: The Classic Account of the Bombing of Pearl Harbor*. New York: Henry Holt & Company, Inc., 2001.

McDonough, Frank. *Hitler, Chamberlain and Appeasement*. New York: Cambridge University Press, 2002.

Manchester, William. *American Caesar: Douglas MacArthur 1880–1963*. New York: Laureleaf, 1996.

Mason, Jr., Herbert M. *The Rise of the Luftwaffe: Forging the Secret German Air Weapons, 1918–1940*. New York: Dial Press, 1973.

Mann, Chris, and Christer Jorgensen. *Arctic War*. New York: St. Martin's Press, 2003.

Murray, Williamson. *Luftwaffe, 1933–45*. Dulles, Virginia: Brasseys, 1996.

Mussolini, Benito, et al. *My Rise and Fall*. New York: Da Capo Press, September 1998.

Nardo, Don (ed.) *The Rise of Nazi Germany*. San Diego: Greenhaven Press, 1999.

Offner, Arnold. *The Origins of the Second World War: American Foreign Policy and World Politics, 1917–1941*. Melbourne, Florida: Krieger, 1986.

Patton, George S. *War As I Knew It*. New York: Mariner Books (Houghton Mifflin), 1995.

Potter, Elmer Belmont. *Nimitz*. Annapolis, Maryland: The Unites States Naval Institute Press, 1988.

Reynolds, David. From *Munich to Pearl Harbor: Roosevelt's America and the Origins of the Second World War*. Chicago: Ivan R. Dee, 2001.

Rommel, Erwin, et al. *The Rommel Papers*. New York: Da Capo Press, 1988.

Rothbard, Murray N. *America's Great Depression*. Auburn, Alabama: Ludwig Von Mises Institute, 2000.

Sharp, Alan. *Versailles Settlement Peacemaking in Paris, 1919* (The Making of the 20th Century). New York: Bedford/St. Martin's Press, 1991.

Smith, Denis Mack. *Mussolini*. New York: Sterling Publications, 2002.

Speer, Albert, et al. *Inside the Third Reich: Memoirs*. New York: Touchstone Books, 1997.

Taylor, A.J.P. *The Origins of the Second World War*. New York: Touchstone Books, 1996.

Thorne, Christopher. *The Approach of War, 1938–1939*. New York: St. Martin's Press, 1967.

Trye, Rex. *Mussolini's Soldiers*. St Paul, Minnesota: Motorbooks International, 1995.

Tucker, Robert C. *Stalin in Power: 1928–1941*. New York: Norton, 1990.

Woodman, Richard. *Arctic Convoys 1941–1945*. London: John Murray Publications Ltd.,1996.

Further Information

BOOKS

Goldstein, Margaret J. *World War II: Europe* (Chronicle of America's Wars). Minneapolis: Lerner Publications, 2004.

Jensen, Richard, and Tim McNeese, ed. *World War II 1939-1945* (Discovering U.S. History). New York: Chelsea House, 2010.

Mara, Wil. *Kristallnacht: Nazi Persecution of the Jews in Europe* (Perspectives On). New York: Marshall Cavendish, 2010.

Ruggiero, Adriane. *American Voices from the Great Depression*. New York: Marshall Cavendish, 2005.

WEBSITES

www.wwiimemorial.com
The U.S. National World War II Memorial.

www.hitler.org
The Hitler Historical Museum is a nonpolitical, educational resource for the study of Hitler and Nazism.

http://gi.grolier.com/wwii/wwii_ mainpage.html
The story of World War II, with biographies, articles, photographs, and films.

www.ibiblio.org/pha
Original documents on all aspects of the war.

DVDS

Great Fighting Machines of World War II. Arts Magic, 2007.

The War: A Film by Ken Burns and Lynn Novick. PBS Home Video, 2007.

World War II 360°. A & E Television Networks, 2009.

Index

Page numbers in **bold** refer to photographs or illustrations. WWI refers to World War I.